Relational Discipleship

Mentoring with Confidence

Relational Discipleship

Mentoring with Confidence

Kyle Vens

© 2023 by Kyle Vens

All rights reserved. No part of this book may be reproduced in any form without permission in writing from the publisher, except in the case of brief quotations embodied in critical articles or reviews.

Scripture quotations, unless otherwise indicated, are taken from the Holy Bible, New International Version®, NIV®. Copyright © 1973, 1978, 1984, 2011 by Biblica, Inc.™ Used by permission. All rights reserved worldwide. www.zondervan.com The "NIV" and "New International Version" are trademarks registered in the United States Patent and Trademark Office by Biblica, Inc.™

Scripture quotations marked ESV are from The ESV® Bible (The Holy Bible, English Standard Version®), copyright © 2001 by Crossway, a publishing ministry of Good News Publishers. Used by permission. All rights reserved.

Edited by Emily Gehman; Design by Kevin Mungons

ISBN:979-8-3893-2168-7

Contents

Introduction	7
1. You Can Do This!	13
2. What Does It Mean to Be a Disciple?	27
3. Who is the Best Fit?	41
4. Jesus' Model of Discipleship	55
5. Paul's Approach to Discipleship	67
6. Big Picture Goals	75
7. The Process of Change	87
8. A Few Guidelines	97
9. The Search Begins	113
10. Finding Your X	127
11. Digging For Treasure	143
12. When You Hit A Rock	155
13. Striking Gold	165
14. Reaping the Reward	191
Conclusion: Let's Go!	209
Notes	211
Acknowledgments	217
Chart	218

INTRODUCTION

The Big Problem

You do not need this book to start discipling someone!

That might seem like a weird way to begin a book about discipleship, but it's true. Reading this book will not certify you as an equipped discipler. No book can do that; the only thing that can ever make you an effective discipler is the Holy Spirit. You already have the ability to start investing in the life of someone today—don't rely on this book.

Don't be like me. Do not sit on the sidelines waiting for a book or course to equip you to disciple. Start investing in someone today.

More often than I'd like to admit, I have looked toward curricula and benchmarks before discipling. I've been afraid of being ill-equipped, and consequently did not take the opportunity to disciple. There have been moments where I've watched God-given opportunities slip away because I was afraid I would not be enough, and God would not be able to use me. My fear of being ill-equipped suppressed the Holy Spirit's voice and my willingness to disciple.

I remember one person who was the perfect candidate

for me to mentor. I invited him to a weekend retreat with a campus ministry I was a part of, and on Saturday night, after a call to faith, he gave his life to the Lord! His newfound belief made him hungry to learn more. He was excited to start studying Scripture with me, and I had the perfect opportunity to lead him through the basics of the gospel, but I did not. Instead, I avoided spiritual conversations with him and rarely connected, and slowly but surely, I watched my opportunity to help him grow in his faith slip through my fingertips. I did not act because I was afraid—afraid I wouldn't have the right answer, or I'd let him down in some way. I let the opportunity pass by, and he remained young in the faith. My fear held me back from discipleship and impacted the spiritual health of another believer.

Don't be like me.

Fear

Fear is one of the primary reasons people hesitate to disciple others. So let's talk about it.

There are two different types of fear that everyone experiences: external fear and internal fear. External fears are caused by outside sources: the scary clown, your airplane in turbulence, or a rollercoaster. External fears are common and assist our body's decision to run or fight the fear. External fears are no fun, but for the most part, do not interfere with our daily lives.

Internal fears, on the other hand, can be silent killers. Internal fears come from within oneself. This fear is the little voice in your head telling you that you can't. Internal fears could be the fear of failure, fear of judgment, or fear of not being good enough. These fears can paralyze us and keep us from taking action. It happens in sports, theater, school, work, relationships, friendships, and even in the Christian mission. In fact, it is possible that your internal fear is the reason you are reading this book. Maybe you're afraid you won't be smart enough, wise enough, funny enough, engaging enough, a good enough listener, or have your life together enough to help someone else.

I'm always reminded of how fear can stop us from taking action in my work as a campus pastor. Every day I have the incredible opportunity to meet and disciple absolutely wonderful college students. The men and women I meet with are some of the most Spirit-filled people I know. They lead college ministries, are strong in their faith, are knowledgeable, and they have the potential to make a huge impact in their communities.

Start now!
You don't need more knowledge or experience or a Bible college degree. You need the Holy Spirit; He will empower you to touch hearts and lives.

But I'm always surprised to hear how many of them don't feel like they know enough or are equipped enough to make a difference in the lives of their classmates. They compare themselves to others and give reasons why they cannot disciple anyone, but a majority of the time it boils down to internal fears.

There are a lot of internal fears, but they all wrestle with one basic question: Am I enough? Am I smart enough? Cool enough? Funny enough? Attractive enough? As we step into talking about what God has called us to in discipleship, I want you to know one essential thing: *you are enough!*

How do I know that? Because you being *enough* has nothing to do with you and everything to do with Jesus.

Jesus Calls the Ordinary

Look at Peter and Andrew in Matthew 4:18–20. They are two uneducated fishermen working with their dad—what could they have to offer Jesus? They didn't have knowledge, wealth, influence, or anything of value for Jesus. But in their ordinariness, Jesus calls them and says, "Come, follow me . . . and I will send you out to fish for people" (Matt. 4:19). Jesus tells them that *He* will make them fishers of men. Jesus is the one who will equip them! He does not expect them to come equipped; He knows it's going to be a journey of growth.

But what do Peter and Andrew do next?

"At once they left their nets and followed Him" (Matt. 4:20). The Scriptures don't even tell us if there was any kind of conversation at all. Wouldn't you have asked some questions before leaving your job in the middle of the day? I would have. But they just got up and left at Jesus' first call. The only criterion Jesus sets for us is faith-driven action. Jesus desires obedience to His call, not knowledge or training or sage wisdom. Just simple obedience. Isn't that beautiful?

Notice Jesus' call to faith-driven action in the great commission: "Then Jesus came to them and said, 'All authority in heaven and on earth has been given to me. Therefore go and make disciples of all nations, baptizing them in the name of the Father and of the Son and of the Holy Spirit, and teaching them to obey everything I have commanded you. And surely I am with you always, to the very end of the age'" (Matt. 28:18–20).

In three sentences Jesus uses five verbs (go, make, baptize, teach, obey) and every single one of them requires faith-driven action! These verbs may sound scary to you, and honestly, they are a little scary. Jesus gives us a big responsibility. But Jesus does not say, "Go and make disciples of all nations . . . Actually, first, make sure you memorize at least fifteen Bible verses and have your life together." Or "make sure you attend a four-year Bible college before sharing the gospel." No, Jesus tells us to go today! This means that all of us—and I mean *all* of us—are commissioned by Jesus regardless of our present knowledge.

But notice what Jesus says in the last sentence: "Surely I am with you always!"

Like when Jesus told Peter and Andrew that He would make them fishers of men, Jesus tells us He will be with us as we step into His calling to fulfill the great commission. Jesus is saying that it is not about us or our knowledge; it's about what *He* will provide for us.

Peter and Andrew are a model of living in faith-driven action. They dive right in, in obedience, with nothing to offer Jesus, trusting Him to equip them. We are to dive in, too, and take hold of the great commission knowing that *He* will equip us also to be "fishers of men" (and for whatever else He calls us to do)!

Consider the disciples' actions after Jesus' ascension. In the great commission, Jesus gives His disciples teaching responsibility (Matt. 28:20). It is the disciples' graduation day! They had been trained and given opportunities to serve and help with Jesus' ministry, and now it was their turn to go and teach the world. The disciples had all of the knowledge—or at least *a lot* more than when they started. If there was ever someone equipped to go and teach others, it was them! Yet, Jesus pumps the brakes on their mission and tells them to wait in Jerusalem until the Holy Spirit comes (Acts 1:4–5). Why? Why would Jesus give the disciples a command to make disciples throughout the world and then ask them to wait? Even though the disciples knew all of Jesus' teaching and lived with Him for three years, Jesus knew they would still be ineffective without the Holy Spirit. The disciples needed the Holy Spirit to be effective in the faith and in their ministry. It is only after the Holy Spirit enters Peter, an uneducated fisherman, that he can boldly proclaim Christ and cite Old Testament texts about Jesus to others (Acts 2:14–36). It is through the Holy Spirit, and only the Holy Spirit, that you are equipped!

Now, it is true that in this book you'll get some training. We'll walk through some foundational ideas about discipleship and mentoring, and give you some pointers and practical tips for mentoring and discipling others. But here's the bottom line: you don't need this book. What you really need is the Holy Spirit.

The foundational truth of discipleship is that it must be guided by the Holy Spirit. All the knowledge in the world does not equate to effective discipleship. Effective discipleship only occurs when we abide in the Holy Spirit. Once that truth gets into your bones and into your heart, you'll find no reason to dwell on your fear. I pray you spend some time meditating on that. Jesus is with you. Trust Him to guide you in the truth!

1

You Can Do This!

Tenth grade. Early August.

My mom signed me up to go to a Christian camp known for its high adventure activities, engaging staff, and entertaining messages. My friends were thrilled to go, but I wasn't. I did not want to go to camp. In fact, I didn't want to do anything. I was depressed, had no desire for anything, and was contemplating taking my own life.

I didn't have a real relationship with God, and my faith was shaky, but a few days before camp started, I prayed. I couldn't think of anything else to do. My prayer was simple: "God, I need you to do something big in my life, because if You don't do something, I'll end it."

I arrived at camp and, right on cue, these energetic and seemingly perfect counselors greeted me. They took my bags and introduced me to my cabin mates. And the next two weeks of my life remain some of the most impactful. The camp delivered on its promises for fun: rock climbing, zip-lining, all the camp things. I made terrific friends who loved me in a way I had never experienced before. By far, the best thing was the night at the campfire when the

Holy Spirit stirred inside my heart. He powerfully showed me God's grace, and at that moment, I surrendered to God. I opened my heart to him, and I was overjoyed in a way I cannot describe. God moved in me, I was changed, and the course of my life completely flipped. God transformed my goals, career dreams, and really, my whole heart.

I was all in for Jesus and wanted to spend every waking moment of my life pursuing Him.

In the early months of my Christian walk, I was on fire for Jesus. Zeal for the Lord consumed me, and I hungered for the Word of God and did everything I could to be more like Christ. My faith grew! But my zeal led to a "holier than thou" attitude. I cut out all of my friends and became judgmental toward family and those around me—even fellow Christians.

The first time I went to my church's youth group, I became angry. I expected them to have the same kind of passion I did! But I quickly realized that most of the guys in my small group were there to just hang out with friends or to get a girlfriend. Frequently, I passionately rambled about how Christians should be all in and not be in a youth group just to meet girls. I spent months and months trying to convince them, but my methods were ineffective. My judgmental attitude and the arguments I started impacted my relationships, and my unbridled passion hindered my ability to be like Christ.

I was on track to become a self-righteous and pompous Christian until I met Cam. He was a little older than me—in his mid-twenties—and he worked with my church's youth group. Cam began mentoring me, and he showed me the world through a different lens and helped me become less judgmental and more loving. He listened patiently to my judgmental rants and helped me see the truth in what I was saying as well as the lies. Cam had a knack for breaking down my walls and getting to the heart of the issue. My friendship with Cam softened my heart and dramatically impacted my relationship with God—and everyone else. I am incredibly thankful for him and the difference he made in my life.

My time with Cam made me fall in love with discipleship. I experienced the joy of meeting one-on-one with a mentor, and I yearned for others to experience even a slice of what I'd had with my mentor. But when I looked at the Christians around me, I saw few discipling relationships. The lack of discipleship broke my heart, and I was perplexed: if discipleship is so important, why is it so uncommon? I set out for answers and asked church leaders about it. They shared their passion for discipleship but also some serious challenges that plague the Church's discipleship efforts.

Discipleship survey

61 % of church leaders say discipleship is *one of* their top priorities.

26 % say it is *the* top priority.

23 % are actually doing it.

According to Barna Research Institute, 61 percent of church leaders say discipleship is one of their church's top priorities, and 26 percent hold it as the top priority[1]. The importance of discipleship has not changed, but the actual percentage of members being discipled is still low. According to the same Barna study, only 23 percent of church members are being discipled. In this context, the definition of discipleship is used loosely, applying it to Sunday school, spiritual mentoring, Bible studies, or Christian book studies as opposed to the traditional sense of one-on-one discipleship. Of the 23 percent of those being discipled, only 17 percent are being discipled in a one-on-one relationship. Only three out of every 100 Christians are being discipled one-on-one! This is a huge discrepancy between the value and the practice of discipleship.

Though many factors play a part in this discrepancy, I see a few major causes. Let's take a look at discipleship in the American church from a 30,000-foot view.

Feed Me, Please

Let's begin with a short visualization exercise.

Visualize a typical Sunday morning at your church. Start from when you turn into the parking lot, and in your mind's eye, go through the order of events until you drive out of the parking lot.

Maybe something like this: You pull into the church parking lot, and maybe a group of helpful volunteers in neon vests direct you to a parking spot. As you enter, a volunteer smiles and opens the door for you and your family. You go through the auditorium doors and quickly find your seat a few minutes before worship begins. When directed, you stand, and if you are brave, you sing to the music led by the church's worship leader. After worship, they pass the donation plates. You listen to the preacher, stand for worship once more, and, after mingling with a few friends, you're back in your car. On the way home, you might reflect on the experience: "Worship was excellent today!" or "I liked the pastor's point on such-and-such." And you move on to the rest of your day feeling "filled."

Does that sound familiar?

What I just described to you is the typical Sunday

morning church service for the modern western church. However, notice something with me: it was strangely similar to going to the movie theater. You were not expected to serve, engage with others, or build meaningful relationships. Rather, you were the consumer. Afterward, you rated the worship, the preaching, and the overall atmosphere. You consumed the church's Sunday morning product and rated it good or bad, or maybe somewhere in between. If, at some point, you don't feel "fed" anymore, you might consider changing churches because you were unsatisfied with the product.

In 2016, Pew Research found the top four qualities Christians consider when shopping for a church: quality of sermons (83%), feeling welcomed by leaders (79%), style of services (74%), and location (70%).[2] Did you notice the consumer language? Church has become a product to be sold, and we are the consumers.

Maybe you're feeling a bit defensive right now. You may believe that's the way the church is supposed to be and, in some ways, you are correct. The church should have a focus on worship (Eph. 5:19), the Lord's supper (1 Cor. 11:17-33), instruction in the Scriptures' teaching, and fellowship (Acts 2:42). There are many aspects of worship the western church does well, and we should praise that—the western church is doing a lot of incredible things for the Kingdom of God!

The problem is the idea of product consumption. It may not be a cash-and-barter system, but many people engage with the church as if it was a product. The church becomes a spiritual gas station to fill up our tank for the week.

A *consumer* is a person who purchases goods and services for personal use. A consumer is expected to consume, not to serve or get involved. Therein lies the problem. The very nature of these interactions is consumer-based. We go to church to receive a product, and if we give it good ratings, we return to receive the same product next week. This looks very different from the early Church in Acts 2, where everyone was expected to be involved. The early church was not led by a singular individual but relied on the entire body to grow and thrive.

> They devoted themselves to the apostles' teaching and to fellowship, to the breaking of bread and to prayer. Everyone was filled with awe at the many wonders and signs performed by the apostles. All the believers were together and had everything in common. They sold property and possessions to give to anyone who had need. Every day they continued to meet together in the temple courts. They broke bread in their homes and ate together with glad and sincere hearts, praising God and enjoying the favor of all the people. And the Lord added to their number daily those who were being saved (Acts 2:42–47).

Look at the engagement of the early Church! They shared what they had, lived in community, and engaged with one another. The congregants gave sacrificially to provide for each other's needs and loved one another deeply. They were not mere consumers but active participants in creating a church community. This is the church we are called to be. It is the difference between going out to eat (consumer) and having a neighborhood potluck (community). You are called not only to receive from the Church but to bring what you uniquely have to the table.

Take a moment and reflect. Have you fallen into the consumer church trap? Do you rely on the church to feed you?

Dietrich Bonhoeffer, a German Lutheran pastor known for his resistance to the Nazis in the 1930s and 1940s, wrote *The Cost of Discipleship*. In it, he commented on the two-tiered models of discipleship, differentiating between "cheap grace" and "costly grace."

Cheap grace is "the preaching of forgiveness without requiring repentance, baptism without church discipline. Communion without confession. Cheap grace is grace without discipleship, grace without the cross, grace without Jesus Christ."[3] In essence, Bonhoeffer says cheap grace is all of the rewards without any of the work. Cheap grace is the grace that many churches have fallen into through this kind of consumerism. As a church focuses on providing a positive experience for its congregation, it risks its ability to preach the entire gospel. Consumeristic churches may struggle to call believers to repent, submit to discipline, or carry their cross.

This type of grace is reflected in what the church emphasizes in its messages. A survey conducted in 2001 asked megachurch (churches with over 2,000 average weekly attendance) congregants what their services focused on, and the top three most prevalent focuses were: God's love and care, personal salvation, and advice for daily living. Now, let me be clear, none of these topics are bad.[4] In fact, all of these topics are important and should be discussed. It is essential for churches to emphasize God's love and practical application to our daily life, but it cannot stop us from talking about more challenging topics like the denial of self, sanctification, and discipleship. Francis Chan comments on what the western church focuses on in his book, *Letters to the Church*. Chan says that it is possible that the American evangelical church may have unintentionally led to an entire generation having a lower view of God as the church pursues a consumer-based church.[5] Chan says our emphasis on the positive, fun, and uplifting has lowered the expectations and responsibilities of believers. Our focus on the positive has hindered our ability to discuss important topics in the faith. If the expectation of the church is to create a fun and entertaining message that caters to the enjoyment of the congregant, then the church will always have trouble talking about "challenging topics" of the faith.

In this model of church, the typical churchgoer will not be exposed to the full breadth of the Christian faith. This type of church culture doesn't create discipleship structures. Discipleship is not an easy task. Discipleship takes work. Discipleship is time-consuming, taxing, challenging, and messy. It's well worth it, but it requires a buy-in that surpasses superficial engagement. Discipleship requires the willingness to dive into life's messiness; the consumer church's focus on engagement does not foster or promote discipleship.

Being a Christian is so much more than agreeing with a set of religious beliefs or a moral code. It's not an American subculture or a demographic label. Being a Christian is about having a relationship with and growing in Christ. Barna describes the evidence of a cheap grace culture like this: "Most Americans who confess their sins to God and ask Christ to be their savior live almost indistinguishable from the unrepentant sinners."[6]

How Does This Affect Discipleship?

Dr. Greg Ogden, former pastor and director of the Doctor of Ministry program at Fuller Theological Seminary, believes that the consumer mentality has greatly impacted the church's ability to disciple. In his book, *Transformational Discipleship: Making Disciples a Few at a Time*, he posits that the consumer models create Christians that are "passive, casual, private, conformed, optional, illiterate (biblically), and inactive."[7]

Consumer-based church models struggle to motivate and activate their church members because they've been indoctrinated in a consumeristic model. It's like walking into a restaurant to eat dinner and being asked to go into the kitchen and start prepping the food. A church taught to consume is unable to produce disciples because discipleship requires effort, action, not just passive consumption. It takes time, energy, and perseverance to be discipled and to disciple others. Discipleship takes intentionality. If church members are taught that church and Christianity is something to be consumed or to "fill them up" for the week, they will resist activities that require work.

The consumer mentality leads to a lackadaisical view of discipleship.

If we follow Christ just for what we can get out of it, our involvement in the work God calls us to will be severely limited. If following Jesus ends at accepting a worldview or a moral code, then the need for believers to be all in disappears. Humanity, and really all of nature, operates by the path of least resistance: all things will travel in the easiest path.[8] Water will always travel downstream. Electrical currents will always move in the easiest direction, and humans will always try to find the easiest way to get what they want. The less effort it takes to get something, the better. The path of least resistance is not always a bad thing. It helps us be effective and get things done—like online shopping! But the path of least resistance becomes a problem when the cost outweighs the gain. For example, the path of least resistance to getting rich is robbing a bank. You may make a lot of money quickly, but the cost is a criminal record and a new semi-permanent home in prison. The cost is greater than the reward.

Congregants will often pursue the path of least resistance as well as long as they receive the reward. This is the pathway of cheap grace—a crown without a cross. The problem with this path is the cost. Cheap grace sacrifices the joy of becoming mature disciples, growing into and using the gifts that God has given us, and hearing "well done my good and faithful servant" (Matt. 25:23). Take a moment and read Matthew 25:14–30. It's clear that the easy route is not worth the cost—just ask the wicked servant.

Barna's research has found that over 40 percent of Christians want to do discipleship on their own.[9] This is a result of the path of least resistance mindset. Discipleship is challenging; it takes a lot of time and effort to disciple someone or to be discipled. So it's easier if we just disciple ourselves. That way, we are still following Christ's command to be discipled, but we can avoid all of the inconvenient effort and accountability. We try to weasel our way out of discipleship because it's hard.

And as a result, discipleship in the American church is suffering.

The good news in all of this? Research shows there are a lot of people who are on the sidelines, longing to get involved in the community, be trained in the faith, take on responsibility, and become effective kingdom workers. Our church members are longing to become equipped and effective disciples. We just need to create cultures to foster that growth. There is an opportunity for discipleship to thrive in the church today, but we must reject the path of least resistance to follow the path to spiritual maturity.[10]

Bonhoeffer calls this path "costly grace." Costly grace is seen in the faith of those we defined as disciples. It is the faith of those who have made Christianity a verb and are actively pursuing Christ. Costly grace is the grace that transforms our minds (Rom. 12:2), kills the flesh (Rom. 8), bears the fruit of the Spirit (Gal. 5:23–24, Matt. 7), and carries our cross (Luke 11). Costly grace says, *I'm all in regardless of what I get out of it*. Costly grace is a faith that embraces discipleship simply because Jesus is worth it. Those seeking to grow in their faith need to grasp costly grace. Then we can truly grow and become mature disciples of Jesus.

I encourage you to ask yourself: Am I following cheap or costly grace? Here's an excerpt from Bonhoeffer's *The Cost of Discipleship* that cuts to the heart of it:

> Costly grace is the treasure hidden in the field; for the sake of it, a man will go and sell all that he has. It is the pearl of great price to buy which the merchant will sell all his goods. It is the kingly rule of Christ, for whose sake a man will pluck out the eye which causes him to stumble; it is the call of Jesus Christ at which the disciple leaves his nets and follows him. Costly grace is the gospel which must be sought

again and again, the gift which must be asked for, the door at which a man must knock.

Such grace is costly because it calls us to follow, and it is grace because it calls us to follow Jesus Christ. It is costly because it costs a man his life, and it is grace because it gives a man the only true life. It is costly because it condemns sin, and grace because it justifies the sinner. Above all, it is costly because it cost God the life of his Son: "ye were bought at a price," and what has cost God much cannot be cheap for us. Above all, it is grace because God did not reckon his Son too dear a price to pay for our life but delivered Him up for us. Costly grace is the Incarnation of God.[11]

I'm convicted every time I read Bonhoeffer's words. I know I do not always measure up to the call of costly grace. There are times where I become apathetic in my faith and passively wait to receive from God. I wait for Him to do something or fill me with his joy and then I will go all in again. There are seasons of my life when I don't spend time intimately with God for weeks or even months at a time. There are times where I fall into consumerism and wait for church to fill me up. I fall short of Jesus' calling all the time, and I constantly need His grace to steer me toward Him.

If you're feeling the same way, it's okay! It's normal to have moments of apathy. It's normal to get distracted. It happens. It only becomes a problem when after we recognize the problem, we remain stagnant. Recognition needs to lead to resolution. When you catch yourself waiting to be filled up by passively attending church, I encourage you to take action. Resist the urge to take the path of least resistance. Reject the consumerism mindset. Receive the call to pursue costly grace. Roll up your sleeves and get ready to do some work.

It will be worth it!

I pray as we take the next steps in our relationship with God and grow in Him, we are able to escape the trap of consumer Christianity. You can make an impact on the kingdom of God and in the lives of those around you! It is going to take work and will require time, effort, and a whole lot of love, but it's worth it. Because when we commit to pursuing costly grace, God will create in us a culture of Christians that are "proactive, disciplined, holistic, transformed, essential, informed, and active."[12]

2

What Does It Mean to Be a Disciple?

In all honesty, I didn't want to transfer.

After two years playing baseball as a student-athlete at Calvin University, I finally had great friends and a good community. I was stepping into my role as the spiritual leader of the baseball team, and God was doing exciting things! Yet there was something inside of me that did not feel right. I asked God why I was feeling this way, and to my shock, I felt God directing me to transfer to Oakland University, a public university near my hometown. I was not thrilled. But I reluctantly followed God's call.

I had no idea what God had in store for me at Oakland, but I knew it was where He wanted me. It didn't take long. A week into the semester, I ran into my friend Cam in the student center.

If you remember, Cam mentored me after I became a Christian, but since I graduated from high school, I hadn't seen him in three years. We caught up and he told me he'd started a ministry that focused on discipleship and leadership development. I was interested in the ministry and thought it would be a good way to get involved on campus and grow as a leader. Within a week, Cam asked me to join. I was not sure what joining his ministry entailed; as far as I knew it just meant spending time with Cam, so I accepted. The more time we spent together, the more involved I became in various ministries, and soon, I became Cam's right-hand man.

One of the best things? Cam and I didn't have an agenda. We didn't have to do anything or talk about anything in particular, we just experienced life together. Sometimes people would ask me if Cam was my mentor, and I never really knew how to respond. It never really felt like mentorship; most of the time, I just followed him around and we talked about life. But as time went on and we continued to meet, I became more like Christ.

Cam *was* discipling me; we just didn't have a name for it. My title was, at best, fluid: sometimes, I was his employee, his volunteer, his coworker. Other times, I was his friend. I wasn't ever just being discipled. I never went to a meeting expecting anything from Cam; I went to spend time with someone who I knew cared about me.

Our friendship was genuine. The ways he found to bring the conversations back to my relationship with Jesus made it a seamless experience. It developed naturally and made our time together meaningful.

And it seemed so different from my perception of discipleship—structured and professional. Saying I was being discipled by Cam felt awkward because discipleship always sounded so formal. Cam showed me discipleship in a different light. It was spontaneous, it lacked structure, and it was relational. I wondered if discipleship meant more than just living life with people.

So, what exactly is discipleship?

Defining Discipleship

Discipleship is one of those churchy words that seems to carry a lot of weight, but no one ever defines. A study done by Barna on discipleship shows a general lack of clarity on the purpose of discipleship. There is a discrepancy between the church layperson and pastors on what discipleship is. The study showed that laypersons tend to be more focused on learning to live a more consistent Christian life (60%), learning to trust in God more (59%) and knowing Christ more deeply (58%), while leaders are more focused on being transformed to be more like Christ (87%), growing in spiritual maturity (79%), and knowing Christ more deeply (78%). None of these answers are bad, but notice the difference in goals between the layperson and the leaders. Laypeople are focused on taking the right actions while leaders are focused on internal transformation. This disconnect between laypeople and leaders may be insignificant, but the lack of clarity can make discipleship goals murky and unobtainable. How can a group of people reach a goal they don't really agree on? Without clear definitions, discipleship ministries struggle, and a general sense of fear leaves people always wondering if they're doing it right.

So first let's take away that fear by starting at the beginning.

God's Call to Discipleship

In Deuteronomy 6, right after receiving the Ten Commandments, Moses gives the Israelites something called the *Shema* (Deut. 6:4–5). The *Shema* is the central instruction to the Jewish nation and is what Jesus quoted when asked about the greatest commandments (see Matt. 22). The *Shema* (vs. 4 and 5) focuses on teaching the next generation:

> Hear, O Israel: The Lord our God, the Lord is one. Love the Lord your God with all your heart and with all your soul and with all your strength. These commandments that I give you today are to be on your hearts. Impress them on your children. Talk about them when you sit at home and when you walk along the road, when you lie down and when you get up. Tie them as symbols on your hands and bind them on your foreheads. Write them on the doorframes of your houses and on your gates.

God commanded the Israelites to share their faith with the next generation so they would know who God is and be right with Him. Notice the practicality: when you sit down, when you walk, when you go to sleep, and when you wake up. They were to know and remember God in their day-to-day actions. For God's people, discipleship and teaching God's commandments were to be done every day.

Discipleship is something that occurs naturally in everyday life. You may not realize it, but you have been discipled your entire life in one form or another. Your parents, teachers, mentors, or even your peers have discipled you and have shaped you into the person you are today.

You know what you know—language, math, cooking, driving, and so on—because someone taught you. You are the product of discipleship in every aspect of your life, and it's likely you haven't even noticed! The process of discipleship happens naturally, and it is central to our physical, mental, emotional, and spiritual development.

For example: I am not a car guy. I am the kind of guy that opens the hood and pretends he knows what's going on when in reality I know next to nothing. When my car breaks down or makes a strange noise, the first thing I do is call my dad. He has more experience, so I rely on my dad's knowledge and expertise to diagnose the problem. My dad has "discipled" me in cars to equip me for the future: He taught me how to change my oil, what to do if my coolant is leaking, how to diagnose basic problems, and so on. My dad discipled me in car maintenance and equipped me with the skills needed to fix it myself . . . or know when to take it to the professionals!

Discipleship
Discipleship is living life with someone and guiding them in the right direction.

If you look closely at your life, you will see the impact of discipleship. Your parents, teachers, friends, coworkers, pastors, and so many more have discipled you into the person you are today. It's part of the natural flow of life; we are in a never-ending process of being discipled and discipling others—whether we acknowledge it or not.

Discipleship in the Christian walk isn't scary. It is, at its essence, living life with someone and guiding them in the right direction.

Defining Discipleship

The word *disciple* comes from the Greek word *mathētēs*, which literally means to be a learner or follower. Specifically, it describes someone who is committed to a significant master. Discipleship was common in the New Testament culture. People pursued formal education in philosophy or religious laws and customs and would seek out a teacher who would instruct them on their journey. These students became groupies as they watched and imitated their masters[1]. Similar to what we do when we choose a college, young men joined various schools each led by a rabbi or religious teachers. Potential students chose what schools or teachers they wanted to "apply" to and then were either accepted or rejected by the teachers. Once accepted, they followed their teacher everywhere and learned everything: stories, habits, traditions, interpretations of the Torah, how they practiced the sabbath, kept commandments, and even what to say in ceremonial situations. Their goal was to become a replica of the teacher.

Disciples also worked to memorize major sections of the Torah as well as their teacher's interpretations of the passage.

First-century disciples imitated the teacher's life and character, and they took this task seriously. A Jewish blessing taken from the Mishna, a book explaining the oral traditions centered around the Torah, says, "Let thy house be a house of meeting for the Sages and sit in the very dust of their feet, and drink in their words with thirst."[2] The disciple should follow the master closely enough to literally be covered in the master's dust as they walked.

Finally, the first-century disciple was expected to raise

up their own disciples. When disciples were fully equipped and graduated from their rabbinical studies, they were expected to start their own rabbinical school and pass along what they learned to the next generation[3].

Take, for example, pre-conversion Paul. Most likely, Saul left home around age 13 to study under Gamaliel, a prominent teacher[4] and well-respected rabbi in Jerusalem (Acts 22:3). He left everything to follow and learn from him: Gamaliel's teaching of the Old Testament, and Gamaliel's ways and traditions.

Jesus' expectations for his disciples were not much different. Except Jesus added a unique twist:

Instead of the disciples choosing Him, Jesus chose them.

Jesus shifts the dynamics. He gives them the choice to follow Him, not the other way around. The people that attended religious schools were the best of the best. Students bound for Harvard and Yale. Yet Jesus didn't choose the cream of the crop. Instead, He chose unexpected disciples: the dropouts and the failures. Jesus chose people who failed out of the religious training before the age of thirteen and had to become fishermen. He chose a ragtag bunch of guys to change the world.

As followers of Christ, we have the privilege of entering discipleship with Him. He is our teacher, and we are His students. As we accept Christ, we submit ourselves to learning from Him and becoming like Him. This is unique to Jesus' discipleship. The cultural understanding of a disciple was to be a follower, a passive observer. But Jesus asks us to be active participants in discipleship. It's the difference between a lecture and hands-on learning. Jesus flips the script, calling them not just to observe Him but to work with Him and thereby become like him: "the student will become like the teacher" (Luke 6:40), and "if you love me, you will keep my commands" (John 14:15). Jesus turns discipleship from passive to active. How exciting! Jesus in His goodness gives us the opportunity to reflect Him. God has entrusted His image and reputation to you! This is a high calling. The responsibility to set a good example of what it means to follow Christ is no easy task. This is what it means to be a disciple.

First-century disciples had expectations placed on them for discipleship. In his book *The Complete Book of Discipleship*, Bill Hull lists five general expectations for disciples[5]:

1) A disciple submits to a teacher who teaches them how to follow Jesus.
2) A disciple learns Jesus' words.
3) A disciple learns Jesus' way of ministry.
4) A disciple imitates Jesus' life and character.
5) A disciple finds and teaches other disciples who also follow Jesus.

Of these five, Hull says most discipleship ministries do well establishing the middle three: learning Jesus' words, way of ministry, and His life and character. But the first and last ones are less practiced. Following expectations, two through four will help us become "better Christians" but leave us on the sidelines of what God calls us to. And really—and slightly ironically—we can't do the middle three without the first and last ones. Failing to submit to a teacher and being unwilling to disciple others describes a culture of Christians who know about the Bible but are not willing to commit to its instructions. Submitting to a teacher and discipling others are essential components of discipleship and Christlikeness.

Being Discipled: "Imitate Me as I Imitate Christ"

In the last few years, I've learned a life-changing, yet incredibly simple principle: If I do not know how to do something, I should ask someone who does! This may seem obvious to you, but to me, it's not. I'm a person known to throw instructions away and then fiddle around with the thing for two hours before consulting a guide. I'm so thankful for all of the wonderful people on YouTube who know how to do everything! These videos offer clear instructions so I can do it myself.

In discipleship, we are instructed to follow someone else's example. Of course, ultimately we are all trying to follow Jesus' example. Jesus tells us in Matthew 23:7-12 that He will always be our central teacher and father, and Jesus tells us to look toward Him always. Jesus actually tells us not to make our own disciples—we are all His disciples! Jesus tells us that we are "brothers" and that He is our instructor. With that said, it's super helpful to have a person, a guide, to help us follow Jesus. Paul writes to the church of Corinth, "imitate me as I imitate Christ" (1 Cor. 11:1). Paul shows us that we need other people who we can tangibly see, be around, and follow, as we all look toward Jesus. It can be difficult to understand and do everything in the Bible. And honestly, Scripture can be confusing! Following the example of someone further along in their journey with Jesus and who knows the Scriptures can help and encourage us as we follow Jesus. They have already walked the trails we are headed down, can help keep us on the right track, and hold us accountable to being like Christ. Their wisdom, experience, and stories help us grow in Christ. Christlikeness is the destination. Every single one of us—mentor and mentee, discipler and disciple—is aiming to be more like Jesus.

Making Disciples: Deliverance, Development, Deployment

Imagine if nobody "new" from now on heard about the gospel. No one was invited to services, churches never held events, and all evangelistic efforts stopped. What would happen to Christianity? Outside of God doing a miracle in the hearts of the nonbelievers, Christianity would stagnate, decline, and eventually die. The spread of Christianity is based on evangelism, and it requires you and me. Jesus has enlisted us to be part of His team to bring people to Him. When you accepted Christ you signed onto His team, and He's given you the task to make and disciple new believers.

You may not think so, but evangelism is a central part of discipleship. In fact, evangelism is the first step in discipleship.

Jesus assigned you the incredible job of making disciples. This job is a privilege: you have been entrusted with helping to save lost souls. Challenges will come, but making disciples is a beautiful opportunity to invest in somebody from a heart of love. Disciple-making is actually a pretty simple process. In Matthew 28:19, we see three hallmarks of disciple-making: deliverance, development, and deployment.

Then Jesus came to them and said,

All authority in heaven and on earth has been given to me. Therefore go and make disciples of all nations, baptizing them in the name of the Father and of the Son and of the Holy Spirit, and teaching them to obey everything I have commanded you. And surely I am with you always, to the very end of the age.

Deliverance. Jesus tells us to make disciples "of all nations"—people from all over the world. Evangelism must be one of the central calls and functions of disciples. Our goal is to find others who need Jesus (everyone), no matter who they are or where they are from, and share Jesus with them.

Development comes from Matthew 28:20, which tells us to teach "them to obey all the commandments I have given you." In development, we help disciples grow by taking the next steps in their relationship with Jesus and build biblical, Christlike character. Development is the heart of discipleship. In discipleship, we refine and become more like Christ.

Deployment is the last step in discipleship. We are not only to equip others but then send them out to make more disciples! Matthew 28:19 tells us to "go and make disciples of all nations." It is important to note that the word "go" does not necessarily entail that you pack your bags and move halfway across the world to share the gospel. For some, that may be the case, but for others, the directive may mean to make disciples in your workplace or neighborhood. James, the brother of Jesus, remained in Jerusalem to lead the church there. He wasn't called to the same mission as Paul, who had the gift of apostleship and was known for church planting. Whether God calls you halfway around the world or in your local neighborhood, the disciple-making directive is clear.

If we have done the work of development correctly and robustly, the disciples we're making will be ready and willing to continue the work by themselves because that is the responsibility of a mature follower.

As we have explored the importance of discipling and being discipled, I hope you have come to see the value in constantly pursuing discipleship expectations. We never graduate from following Jesus! This might feel discouraging to you, but it's actually quite exciting! Discipleship is an action word, and it's a lifelong process. The *ship* suffix in *discipleship* denotes a "state of" or being "contained in." It's an ongoing process, and we're all a part of it for as long as we are alive. It means that Jesus is always with us as we grow in Him, and we can always improve and become more like Him.

Discipleship Is Unique

Discipleship is unique and personal in nature. Everyone has the same goal of being like Christ, but our paths to get there differ. Discipleship will look different in every person. Not all of us need to or will grow in the same ways or at the same rate. Everyone has areas for growth, but those areas are specific to the individual.

For example, I coach a travel baseball team. I love the guys and believe that each player has the potential to be great. But they all have different strengths and weaknesses. One is an incredible hitter but is poor defensively. Another is a terrific outfielder but struggles to hit. Both players are good—great in fact—but they have different things to develop. As the coach, it is my responsibility to work with each one of them on their weaknesses to reach their potential. Likewise, discipleship must be unique and specific to the needs of the individual.

This is where discipleship curriculum falls short. By nature, a one-size-fits-all program cannot meet the needs of the individual. It becomes mechanistic: You start at one end of the program and come out the other end twelve weeks later "discipled." But people aren't programs; everyone is unique. Each disciple is different and needs to grow in different ways. A program that focuses on a specific set of information or character trait, however important it may be, misses the disciples' individual needs. Please hear me: Curriculum isn't bad, it just cannot meet individual needs. A hitting camp for all my baseball players would help them improve their hitting, but it would not meet the needs of those who struggle at defense.

I understand how tempting a programmatic approach can be. A one-size-fits-all curriculum for every believer would be easier! Wouldn't that be cool? A mass-produced training regimen that would equip everyone to be mature in Christ would be wonderful. The reality, though, is that no curriculum, no matter the depth or length, will adequately disciple believers if it is not adapted to the individual. There is value in curriculum, but discipleship that is not personalized to the needs of the individual fails to teach, correct, rebuke, or train adequately.

True discipleship is not a transfer of information but a transformation of the heart[6]. Successful discipleship is measured by the internalization of the material, not in the completion of a packet or course. Programs can produce

Christians who know a lot but whose lives are not changed. Discipleship is a lifetime journey of development, not a 12-week or one-, two-, or even three-year program. We must pull away from the programmatic approach and move to an intimate, Spirit-led friendship between discipler and disciple.

The individuality of discipleship is actually a blessing because it allows discipleship to occur in many contexts and platforms. My time with Cam showed me that discipleship was relational, individualized, and messy at times. But more than anything, it is real.

My time with Cam was relational and God-centered, and it expanded my understanding of discipleship. I encourage the men I disciple to pursue a wide range of discipleship tools. Discipleship must occur within a relational context but there are many tools—small groups, book studies, sermons, and books! You can be discipled by writers or pastors from the other side of the country. Without a regimented structure, there is the freedom to focus on the disciple's needs. What is central to discipleship is the intimacy developed between the mentor and mentee. It is within these relationships that disciplers can truly invest in the disciple, grow with them, focus on their strengths and weaknesses, and teach them to obey Jesus' commands. Give yourself the freedom to create discipleship centered around your unique friendship.

In the next chapter, we'll explore the characteristics of someone who would be a good disciple for you.

3

Who Is the Best Fit?

Stuart and I played on the same baseball team. One day early in the season, our team planned to watch a baseball game at the captain's house after practice. I didn't know Stuart super well at the time, but he asked me for a ride because his car battery died. I did not expect much of our conversation; I thought we'd just talk about baseball and that would take up most of the ten-minute drive.

But Stuart started telling me his life story. I was shocked by his openness. After all, we had only interacted a handful of times up to this moment. When he was done, he asked me what was going on in my life. In a moment of vulnerability, I shared some of my struggles, and he listened. Our ten-minute car ride turned into an hour-long conversation about life. That night Stuart and I became inseparable best friends.

Stuart and I pushed each other to be the best versions of ourselves. We competed on the baseball field, in school, and in just about anything else you could think of. Stuart was my equal and made me a better man because of it.

Maybe you've had a friend like Stuart, too. Someone

who pushes you to be the person they know you can be. These are friends to be cherished—but not people you should mentor.

It may be tempting to try and mentor a friend because it seems like an easy transition. But although your intention may be good, it could get complicated. Altering the dynamics of an established friendship into a mentor-mentee relationship can put unnecessary tension on the relationship.

This brings up an interesting question, though. If mentoring a friend is off the table, who are you supposed to mentor? How do you know who will be a good fit? How do you know who will become a friend, mentee, or just an acquaintance? In short, there is not a definitive answer; it's a case-by-case basis. There's no formula for finding the perfect mentee because everyone is unique. But there are clues to help you decide if your potential mentee will be a good fit.

Signs of a Not-So-Good Fit

You Are in a Similar Stage of Life

A tell-tale sign that the person you are thinking of mentoring is not a good fit is if they are in a similar stage of life with you. Let's explore the disciples' relationships with one another. Jesus called the disciples from various backgrounds: fishermen, tax collectors, zealots, and even some professions we don't know about[1]. It was truly a diverse group. Some were well educated, like Matthew (Matt. 9:9); others were not (Matt. 4:16–20). Members held different political beliefs: Simon the zealot was a political activist bent on overthrowing the Roman government, while

Matthew was a tax collector, working with the Roman government. Jesus truly chose a diverse group. But they all had one thing in common: they were all in a similar stage of spiritual maturity. All of the disciples had similar knowledge of the Torah when Jesus called them. None had a background in religious training, and they were all on even footing with one another. Because the disciples were in similar stages of life it would have been challenging, even disastrous, for them to mentor each other.

Discipleship is based on the premise that there is a teacher and a student, implying a difference in knowledge or understanding of a subject. One is expected to learn from the other. If you are in a similar position of life with someone else, trying to establish a mentoring relationship could be risky. Both of you are still trying to figure it out. It's probably better for you to remain friends and push each other toward Christ.

You Argue with Them

Stuart and I competed in everything we did. From school to ping pong to who would have a better baseball career, we went head-to-head. Our rivalry led to spirited arguments that left us heated at times. I loved these moments with him because they were real—just two guys trying to beat each other out. If you find yourself in moments where you are unsure of who is further along emotionally, spiritually, or in leadership qualities, it may be a good indication that they are in the friend category and not a potential mentor or mentee. Relationships naturally settle into unspoken relational dynamics. In some relationships, there's an unspoken understanding that one person knows more or is more developed.

In Mark 9, we see the disciples "secretly" argue about who is the greatest among them.

> He said to them, "The Son of Man is going to be delivered into the hands of men. They will kill him, and after three days he will rise." But they did not understand what he meant and were afraid to ask him about it. They came to Capernaum. When he was in the house, he asked them, "What were you arguing about on the road?" But they kept quiet because on the way they had argued about who was the greatest (Mark 9:31-34).

The disciples did not ask Jesus about the bomb He just dropped. Why the disciples have this argument is unclear, but I hypothesize it was prompted by failed opportunities for each to assert himself as the leader. In the chapter's previous story, the disciples couldn't heal a demon-possessed boy[2]. It was a chance for each disciple to prove his worth and separate himself from the others, but they all failed. As the disciples argued about who was the greatest, they ironically placed themselves in similar positions with each other—it solidified their status as equals.

The unclear relational dynamics created tension between them. It would have been ill-advised for Peter to try to mentor James after that. If the dynamics of your relationship have not become clear naturally or you find yourself arguing who is further along, it's likely that you are in too similar a position for a mentoring relationship.

You Have a Similar Understanding of Scripture

Throughout the Gospels, the disciples show similar

levels of understanding of Jesus' words. No one stepped up and saw things from a higher point of view. Sure, Peter had his moments, but he also got corrected more than any of the disciples. The disciples were in a state of growth together, and continually showed themselves to have a similarly limited understanding of Jesus' teachings. All of the disciples are commonly confused by Jesus' parables, even to the point of Jesus's frustration[3]. None of them were in a position to offer counsel or understanding to each other. It's challenging to learn from someone who knows as much as you—imagine learning math from someone who knows just as much math as you. To use an old adage, it's the blind leading the blind! Being in a similar stage of biblical understanding may indicate that you'd both be better off remaining friends.

The Relational Dynamics Don't Work

Relationship dynamics naturally set themselves. How we interact, communicate, and work with others happens naturally through the exploration of the relationship. For example, if you were to meet your favorite celebrity, the relationship would most likely consist of you gawking at them, asking questions, and taking photos. On the other hand, the way you and your best friend communicate with each other is much different: without filters, back and forth banter, and less gawking. These dynamics happen naturally; neither scenario is discussed beforehand. It just happens.

As you think about your potential mentee, you should be looking for dynamics that are typically focused on them, ones where you are offering counsel and support and answering questions about life. These are excellent dynamics of the right kind of discipleship relationship.

Signs of a Good Fit

You See the World through a Different Lens

I love the way Jesus teaches His disciples. He helps them see the world from a different perspective. Throughout Jesus' ministry, He and the disciples were continually presented with potentially intimidating situations. They met with religious leaders, social misfits; they raised the dead, healed people, fed them, and taught them. The disciples handled these situations with varying degrees of success, but generally, they were focused on the present moment, slightly near-sighted. Jesus, on the other hand, sees the bigger picture. In Mark 8:31–33, we see Peter's short-sightedness.

> Then He began to teach them that the Son of Man must suffer many things and be rejected by the elders, chief priests, and scribes, and that he must be killed and after three days rise again. He spoke this message quite frankly, and Peter took him aside and began to rebuke him. But Jesus, turning and looking at his disciples, rebuked Peter and said, "Get behind Me, Satan! For you do not have in mind the things of God, but the things of men" (Mark 8:31–33).

Peter actually tried to rebuke Jesus! It is likely that he was scared, didn't understand what Jesus was saying, and feared what would happen to himself if Jesus died. Peter focused on their present safety. But Jesus rebuked Peter directly. He wasn't focused on the moment but saw the situation from a different perspective—the salvation His death and resurrection would secure. Jesus helped the disciples see things from an entirely new perspective.

Helping someone process and see things from a different perspective is a key role in mentoring. It's a great sign you are in a position to mentor that person.

They Ask You to Rejoice with Them

Luke 10:1–23 is one of my favorite Bible passages. Jesus sends out seventy-two disciples on a short-term mission trip. He provided them with specific instructions on what they were to do and how they should behave. When the disciples returned, they were ecstatic. They said, "Lord, even the demons submit to us in your name" (vs. 17). What an incredible experience that must have been! They were given the power to drive out demons and perform miracles, and they began to use the gifts God gave them. And Jesus rejoiced with them—Jesus joined in the excitement!

> At that time Jesus rejoiced in the Holy Spirit and declared, "I praise you, Father, Lord of heaven and earth, because you have hidden these things from the wise and learned, and revealed them to little children. Yes, Father, for this was well-pleasing in your sight. All things have been entrusted to me by my Father. No one knows who the Son is except the Father, and no one knows who the Father is except the Son and those to whom the Son chooses to reveal him."

> Then Jesus turned to the disciples and said privately,

'Blessed are the eyes that see what you see. For I tell you that many prophets and kings desired to see what you see but did not see it, and to hear what you hear but did not hear it'" (Luke 10:21–24).

When others come to you with their success, rejoice with them! Rejoice in their success, no matter how big or small. When people come to you excited with news it usually means they value your opinion and want you to celebrate with them. It is a sign of trust and respect. Jesus affirmed to the disciples that they were blessed and special. Personal and direct affirmation is crucial; being affirmed by someone you respect is so meaningful! When people share success with you, rejoice with them and affirm their character. This is a great sign this relationship can turn into discipleship.

They Want to Imitate You

As you grow in your maturity in Christ and are transformed by His radical love, there will likely be moments where someone says to you, "I wish I was like you" or even "I was trying to decide what to do, and I asked myself 'what would [your name] do?'" Statements like these may make you feel uncomfortable, awkward, or like they're seeing you in an unhealthy way[4], it is more likely because they see Christ in you. Paul instructs the church in Corinth to "Follow my example, as I follow the example of Christ.[5]"

If someone looks up to you and tries to imitate you, there is a good chance that a mentoring relationship can be formed.

The examples listed above are just a few practical ways to determine whether or not someone is a good fit to start mentoring. There is no formula to figure out if you can mentor someone, and sometimes it takes trial and error. Honestly, mentor-mentee relationships come down to goodness-of-fit. Not all relationships will work, and sometimes you simply have more rapport with someone than another. The best way to see if the relationship will work is by getting to know them. There is no pressure to establish yourself as their mentor or vice versa. Allow the relational dynamics to play out naturally, and then go from there.

Logistical Considerations

Determining who is a good fit for you to mentor is up to your discretion. It may take a few test runs. In order to avoid potential confusion, here are a few general guidelines:

A good mentoring fit

Do not mix genders. In Titus 2:3-5, Paul implies same-gender discipleship roles as he implores the older women to disciple the younger women, and older men to disciple younger men. Maintaining

- Don't mix genders.
- Consider the age gap.
- Choose teachable mentees.
- Consider schedules, location.
- Be cautious of mentoring people you live with.

boundaries between genders not only protects our hearts but allows for deeper conversations. On a practical level, it generally doesn't make sense for a woman experiencing menopause to seek counsel from a male pastor. If needed, mixed-gender mentoring relationships can occur, but they can only go so deep; boundaries of conversation topics and meeting settings should be explicitly stated at the outset. Appropriate topics boundaries must be maintained, and mixed-gender discipleship relationships should never meet in a private setting where there is no accountability.

These guidelines exist to protect both parties, not under the assumption that anything inappropriate will happen.

Be cognizant of the age gap. There are no true requirements for an age gap between mentors and mentees, but it is something to consider. If your mentee is the same age as you or older you may have trouble establishing credibility. They may view you as an equal and you will have trouble challenging your mentee when needed. In addition, if there is too big of an age gap, there may be a generational disconnect that makes starting the relationship awkward. Use your discretion to determine whether the age gap works for you and your mentee.

Mentees must be teachable. There's no value in trying to teach someone who is unteachable. If the person you are considering mentoring is hard-headed and unwilling to consider others' thoughts, it is unlikely they will be a good mentee—for anyone, not just you.[6]

Consider schedules and location. Mentoring takes time and intentionality. If your schedules do not mesh, you'll spend your entire relationship playing phone tag. And it's difficult (though not impossible) to mentor someone who is not in your area. Finding someone local offers more opportunities to see each other and allows them to see you interact in real life.

Be cautious of mentoring people you live with, like family members or roommates. Taking care of your family is essential,[7] but this doesn't mean you have to mentor them. You risk putting serious stress on a relationship by introducing formal mentoring. If you are going to specifically mentor your child (beyond parenting), sibling, or roommate, they have to be open to it. If they're not interested, respect that. Don't argue, but connect them with someone in a local church. Mentoring roommates can create an unhealthy relationship where both parties feel watched or judged.

Know Yourself

Understanding your own strengths and weaknesses can help you make an informed decision on who to mentor. And it will allow you to better help the other person grow. If you're mentoring someone you know has low self-confidence, being an encourager could be a great fit. On the other hand, if you're mentoring someone who struggles with arrogance, being an encourager could be counterproductive.

You may feel awkward listing your strengths, but do so with Scriptural humility: In Romans 12:3, Paul says, "for by the grace given me I say to every one of you: Do not think of yourself more highly than you ought, but rather think of yourself with sober judgment, in accordance with the faith God has distributed to each of you." Paul says to avoid hubris by not thinking too highly of yourself. This also implies that we should not think of ourselves as more lowly, either. Rather, we should think of ourselves with a "sober mind"—this means seeing *both* your strengths and weaknesses.

It's important that we see ourselves clearly. If you lack this skill, you are unable to invest in others to your full potential. If you see yourself as more highly than you are and try to mentor someone who is actually similar to you or more developed, it is likely tension will build and the relationship will collapse. However, if you view yourself too lowly, you may feel ill-equipped for mentoring someone who might need you. As you think about people you would like to mentor, be honest with yourself about who you are. Take a few moments right now to identify five of your strengths and five weaknesses. You'll get clarity and a better sense of who you can begin mentoring.

Strengths	Weaknesses

If you're having trouble identifying your strengths and weaknesses, ask a trusted friend to give an honest assessment. It may be challenging to hear their feedback, but it will help you grow. I would rather be hurt by a friend through honest critique than to be encouraged by a lie.[8] A friend's honesty is a good way to gauge your strengths and weaknesses; spend time reflecting on what they say.

As you begin seeing yourself in a sober light, embrace your strengths and be humbled by your weaknesses. Know what you bring to the table so you can give your best to the relationship.

Stay with Faithful Friends

I'm grateful for the mentors in my life who have so faithfully invested in me. They have been a true blessing. But

I am also grateful for my friends who have stayed friends over the years. There's no pressure to turn every relationship into a discipleship relationship. Friendships are essential to our success and growth in the faith. I credit a lot of my high school junior and senior years' success to Stuart and his friendship, and I am truly grateful for him. He invested in me in some incredible ways. Stuart was there when I was hurting, when I was happy, and everything in between. Our friendship was mutually beneficial—we both grew together and invested in each other. If you have a friend like that, hold them tightly. There is true joy in such a friendship.

4

Jesus' Model of Discipleship

I was completely embarrassed.

The first time I spoke for Young Life, I was confident that I was going to crush it. I walked cockily to the front of the room with my PowerPoint at the ready. I had just boasted to the Young Life president that I was an excellent public speaker, and honestly, I thought it was true until I got to the podium. I froze. I saw all the faces looking at me and all my swagger disappeared immediately. I delivered what was quite possibly the most monotone and dry message of all time.

I left that night ashamed. I felt inadequate and knew I needed help. I reached out to a couple mentors, Dale and Cam, to teach me how to create and give engaging messages. They taught me the basics, and over time, I slowly but surely learned methods of faithful message preparation. My messages did not improve overnight; every week for the next six months, I delivered slightly better messages, and although they were still far from the models I was shooting for, I was slowly getting there.

I always appreciated the wisdom I got from Dale and Cam because they did not just tell me what to do, they equipped me to do it. Instead of giving me a one-size-fits-all model, they gave me a general structure and the tools needed to create a good message. It has been years since my first message at Young Life, but I still refer to these tools when I prepare to speak. I've created my own style of teaching, but without this foundation, Young Life would have had to suffer through many more dry messages, and I would not have developed the love for preaching I have today.

Whether it be speaking, changing a flat tire, baking, or discipleship, we can learn from people who've already done it! The key to a good model is that it equips us with skills, not only the ability to complete a task.

Equipping people with skills instead of programs is the key to discipleship because everyone is unique. Your interactions with your mentees differ between the people you meet with; discipleship is unique to each person, and it's impossible to create a model of discipleship that fits everyone. This means that no model can perfectly equip us for our relationship with our mentees, including this book.

Different, but Helpful

The Bible doesn't give us step-by-step formulas. But we do have models of discipleship. The New Testament gives us two extensive examples of discipleship: Jesus and Paul. Both spent significant time with their disciples and aimed to help their disciples become like Jesus. They don't give us a step-by-step process, but their models give us insight into discipleship that will help us disciple others. Neither model is complete—and that's okay because discipleship must be fluid and adaptable to each person—but both offer good guides to follow. Your relationships will not necessarily fit these models perfectly. Don't worry! It's all part of the process. The goal of a model is to be a frame of reference, not to tell you what to do in every situation.

When you need help

Whether it be speaking, changing a flat tire, baking, or discipleship, we can learn from people who've already done it!

Think of this view of New Testament discipleship as a 30,000-foot view. For a more detailed study of each model, check out Greg Odgen's book, *Transforming Discipleship*, where Ogden terrifically breaks down and explains these models.

Jesus' Discipleship

Jesus models for us the importance of keeping an end goal in mind. Jesus knew He was destined for the cross and He only had three years to prepare the disciples to carry on His mission. Jesus' clear goal informed how He discipled His students. Jesus' model[1] is ideal if your goal is to train your disciple for a specific role like teaching, administration, or taking over a position.

The model of discipleship that Jesus demonstrates breaks down into four stages known as the situational leadership model.

Stage one: Jesus, the Living Example—The disciples watched and absorbed Jesus' teaching.

Stage two: Jesus, the Provocative Teacher—Jesus dislodged faulty ideas and created a kingdom mindset mentality.

Stage three: Jesus, the Supportive Coach—Jesus sends the disciples out and leads a supportive debrief on the disciples' mission trip.

Stage four: Jesus, the Ultimate Delegator: After the resurrection, He empowers them to go and continue His mission.

The Prepatory Empowerment Process of Jesus

	Pre-disciple	Stage 1	Stage 2	Stage 3	Stage 4
Jesus' role	Inviter	Living example	Provocative teacher	Supportive coach	Ultimate delegator
Disciples' role	Seekers	Observers and imitators	Students and questioners	Short-term missionaries	Apostles
Readiness level	Hungry to know whether Jesus was Messiah	Ready to observe who Jesus is and the nature of His mission	Ready to interact with Jesus, publicly identify with Him	Ready to test the authority of Jesus to work through them	Ready to assume full responsibility for making and reproducing disciples
Key questions	Is Jesus the Messiah?	Who is Jesus, and what is His ministry and mission?	What is the cost of following Jesus?	Will the power of Jesus work through us when we take on His ministry?	Will I give my life entirely to the mission of making reproducing disciples?

Stage One: Jesus the Living Example

Stage one is the "I do; you watch" stage.[2] In this stage, the primary role of the discipler is to set an example for the disciple to observe. Jesus continually set an example for His disciples through His way of living and His authority. Before becoming involved in Jesus' ministry, the disciples witnessed Jesus' teaching, interactions with religious leaders, and power over demonic forces.[3] The disciples' role was to soak it all in. The disciples watched Jesus and became familiar with Him.

In this stage, you want to be intentional in inviting your disciple to join you in processes and activities. If your goal is to train them as teachers, it may mean inviting them to watch you prepare or practice your messages. If your goal is to equip your disciple to evangelize, you may ask them to join you and watch you interact with others. You cannot take a passive approach with them. Pursue them and find opportunities to interact with them.

As I approached my senior year at Oakland University, I knew I would need to teach someone else how to prepare and give messages so the next generation at Young Life would be successful. So I began meeting with Hunter, and as we spent time together, he watched me prepare messages and I would walk him through it: I shared aloud how I studied and consulted different commentaries to gain insight into passages. Hunter's role in the process was to soak in what he saw and heard. Over time, Hunter began to naturally pick up on the flow of a message and began offering suggestions and his own opinions as he grew more confident. Though I could have felt threatened by that, I am thankful God gave me the grace to respond positively!

When this happens to you, encourage your mentee to offer their opinions and even ask for them. As your disciple becomes more confident, you will find yourself naturally transitioning to the second stage of Jesus' model of discipleship: The Provocative Teacher.

Stage Two: Jesus the Provocative Teacher

Stage two can be explained simply as the "I do; you help" stage. In this stage, your job is to invite your disciple to help you and to ask them questions that will further their thinking. Inviting your disciples into your work helps bridge the gap between watching and doing. It moves the disciple from a passive to an active participant. Jesus is a provocative teacher in Luke 9:3-17 when He asks His disciples to become active participants in His ministry.

In this famous story of feeding 5,000 hungry people, Jesus shifts the disciples' mindsets. At this point, the disciples were only passively involved in ministry. They had observed Jesus moving and doing incredible things but had not yet been involved in the action. When confronted with an approaching challenge—5,000 hungry people—the disciples did the reasonable thing and told Jesus to make the crowd leave so they could find food and shelter. This wasn't a bad plan, but it was a passive plan.

In this moment, Jesus did something important; He invited the disciples into active ministry. He put it on them, saying, "You give them something to eat." Rather than send the people away, Jesus used it as an opportunity to get His disciples involved. The disciples, stunned and stuck in passive ministry, complained that it was too difficult[4]. They were still living in passive ministry. They neither trusted in the Lord nor believed they were capable of this responsibility. Jesus invited them to be a part of His miracle, moving them from passive observers to active participants. Notice how Jesus gave clear instructions: manage the crowd and distribute the food[5]. As the provocative teacher, Jesus used this stage to give disciples responsibility without crushing them in the process.

Like Jesus, you can use this stage to help your disciple move from passive observers to active participants. Yes, it takes effort and can begin by asking thought-provoking questions or by creating ways for them to help. I asked Hunter strategic questions to help him think more deeply about message preparation. We had conversations about his views on teaching styles and what he thought was best, and I welcomed his contributions. These moments helped Hunter transition from someone passively pursuing speaking to actively engaging in it.

As your disciple takes first steps in being an active participant in the faith, be sure to encourage them. They are in a fragile state and should not be burdened with tasks beyond their capability. As they grow in confidence, you will transition to the next stage of Jesus' model of discipleship.

Stage Three: The Supportive Coach

This is the "You do; I help" stage. As the disciples grew in their understanding of Jesus and stepped further into His ministry, Jesus transitioned from the provocative teacher to the supportive coach.

Jesus as the supportive coach is seen best in Luke 10, where He sends seventy-two followers on a short-term mission trip. Their goal was to spread the gospel to neighboring towns and tell them that "the kingdom of God is near."[6] Although it doesn't explicitly say the seventy-two were nervous or felt unequipped, it's not unreasonable to think they didn't feel entirely prepared for the journey. Just look at the briefing Jesus gives them: "Don't bring anything"[7]; "Rely on others to take care of you"[8]; "I am sending you out like lambs among wolves."[9] I would have been terrified! Maybe not one of Jesus' best pep talks.

But His instructions are direct, clear, and concise. Jesus gives direct instructions, appropriate responsibility, and clear expectations. He told them to travel light, heal the sick, proclaim the kingdom of God, and rebuke those who rejected them. Providing your disciple with clear instructions is pivotal to their success. Without clear instructions, disciples are left trying to figure out what to do, and if they're forced to grow too quickly or without clarity, the weight of the responsibility may cause them to stumble.

I've dropped the ball in this category more than I like to admit. I was the head of an outreach program for young adults, and every week I led a team of volunteers to walk around campus and invite people to our event. I was responsible for training and giving them clear instructions, but I didn't do either. I sent them to go talk to people with no understanding of what to do. Thirty minutes later when I checked on them, they'd only been talking with their friends the entire time. I remember being furious with them; I felt like they didn't care about volunteering or the ministry. But my anger wasn't justified. I couldn't be upset that they failed when I didn't tell them the goal. Without clear instructions, your disciple will lack direction and struggle to complete the activity.

Jesus gave clear expectations for the disciples so they would understand what was required of them. Give your disciples direct instructions and clear expectations. And then give them responsibility.

Jesus gave His disciples the authority to heal others and proclaim God's kingdom wherever they went. By providing your mentees with clear authority or responsibility, they gain a better understanding of their role and feel the weight of the responsibility.

Hunter and I met to work on his message preparation and public speaking skills, and I provided Hunter with straightforward instructions, authority, responsibility, and clear expectations. As Hunter practiced and felt the weight of public speaking, he grew as a leader and learned to handle responsibility.

As your disciple grows, they will gain confidence and competency and will be less reliant on you. Make yourself available, but as they develop, allow them to wrestle with ideas on their own so they continue to mature.

Stage Four: Jesus, the Ultimate Delegator

This final stage is the "You do; I watch" stage. In this stage, you step back and allow your disciple to do the majority of the work. As the observer, you get to encourage your disciple when they do something right and be there to answer questions along the way.

How close you and your disciple work together in this stage should be determined by the disciple. They are the ones carrying the weight of the work now and need to make the role their own and feel confident they're doing the right thing. As your disciple grows, give them space to succeed or fail. Allow them the freedom to work, to make and fix mistakes on their own. Don't be too quick to jump in and save the day; that may feel helpful in the moment, but it doesn't help them grow.

In the garden of Gethsemane, Jesus spends some of His final hours praying for His disciples: for their protection, their joy, and their holiness.[10] He also prays a transitional prayer, saying, "as you have sent me into the world, so I have sent them into the world."[11] Jesus has effectively handed the keys to the disciples. It was the disciples' time to carry on Jesus' mission.

Jesus demonstrated the importance of training leaders and releasing them into their communities.

Today, Hunter is a confident and capable public speaker who no longer needs me to help him prepare his messages. Occasionally he asks me to double-check a section for him, and that is okay! I want him to know I'm available for help; even in the delegator stage, we need to be there to support them.

An Overview of Jesus' Model

Jesus' model of discipleship is clear and easy to follow. Jesus had a specific plan for his disciples: to get them ready, in three years, to carry out His mission. Jesus' end goal dictated the way He interacted with His disciples. He modeled how to live, invited them to help in ministry, gave them authority, and finally handed off His ministry to them. If you have an end goal or specific timeframe with your disciple, Jesus' model of discipleship may be a good approach to consider.

If that's not you, that's totally okay! Not every discipleship relationship is going to look the same, and not every relationship fits structurally into the transitional relationship of Jesus' model.

This model of discipleship is effective in relationships that are time intensive. The transitional stages—from "I do; you watch" all the way to "you do; I watch"—takes time. Jesus spent three years with His disciples modeling the life He wanted them to live. Jesus' model usually requires close proximity to your disciple, but with the development of technology, it is possible to do it over long distances if you are intentional. Jesus demonstrates a powerful and replicable model of discipleship, but His model is not the only model of discipleship we have in the New Testament. Paul offers us a generalizable model of discipleship that can be applied to a variety of contexts, focusing on growing in the faith rather than being equipped for a task. We'll look at Paul's model next.

5

Paul's Approach to Discipleship

Remember how I said I always called my dad when I had car trouble? He knows way more about cars than I do, so he is my first phone call when it comes to cars. But here's the thing: He never sat me down and gave me an entire class in car repair 101. He still knows more than I do, but our relationship is one where I know I can call him at a moment's notice.

Jesus' model of discipleship was for a certain period of time (three years) for a specific task (carrying out His ministry), and it came with a lot of watching, a lot of doing, and plenty of instruction. Discipleship 101. But Paul's model of discipleship was different. It was less about a specific task and more about a relationship—one where Paul would be there to answer questions as they arose. Kind of like my dad with the cars.

The best way to describe Paul's approach to discipleship is spiritual parenting. Paul focused on helping the young church understand who they were in Christ and what it meant to live as a Jesus follower—growing up in Christ and being transformed into Christlikeness.

As we look at Paul's model of discipleship, notice it's universal: Every one of us is in the process of growing in Christ. We're all aiming to become more mature in the faith. Because of this, Paul's method of discipleship can be altered to reach people at any step of their Christian journey.

There are four steps in Paul's model: infancy, childhood, adolescence, and adulthood. Each step requires something different from the mentor and pushes the mentee in a unique way.

It's important to note that, just like human development, growing from spiritual infancy to adulthood takes time. You can't blow through these stages in a couple weeks. Reaching spiritual adulthood is a long, challenging, and even sometimes awkward process. But you can't rush it! Respect the time it takes for someone to grow in maturity. It would be unwise to feed a newborn solid food. You have to move slowly from milk to mashed foods to simple foods, and so on and so forth. But you cannot give a baby milk forever; eventually, you need to start feeding them solid food.

The important part is not where your disciple starts, but if they are growing.

Stage One: Infancy—Imitation

If you have kids or are simply a fan of kids, then you are probably familiar with the imitation game parents play with their babies. Parents make a sound or action, and the baby tries to mimic it. Besides being fun and absolutely adorable, this game serves a purpose in the child's development of verbal, motor, and social skills. It is through imitation games that children understand the world around them. The Social Learning Theory[1] hypothesizes that we all learn within a four-step process. Attention (watching and listening), retention (processing the information), reproduction (attempting to copy a behavior), and motivation (external reinforcement). It's through these steps that children come to learn new things.

Eventually, the baby begins to act out of self-motivation rather than imitation.

Paul begins his spiritual empowerment model of discipleship with these same forms of imitation. In 1 Corinthians 11, Paul says, "be imitators of me, as I am of Christ."[2] The first step in Paul's model is to imitate someone as they imitate Christ. By observing someone else, we are able to see how to speak and behave. As a mentor, it is important that you model following Christ in the early stages of your relationship. Your mentee will notice the way you handle yourself and try to model the way you act. As they aim to imitate you and ultimately Christ, make sure that what they are noticing, retaining, and reproducing lines up with Scripture.

As your disciple tries to imitate you, it's inevitable that you will make a mistake—you're not perfect! When you do, be sure to admit it. Your mentees can learn a lot about what it means to follow Christ and forgive as you admit mistakes. And they will start to do the same thing. Allow your disciple space to practice new behaviors, be patient when they fail, and encourage them when they do well. With any new thing, change does not come without setbacks, so be ready to help them as they navigate new terrain.

Stage Two: Identification—Childhood

As a child grows up and learns the appropriate ways to behave, they learn to identify with things. They begin to find out who they are. This time period is one of the most formative stages—it's when children develop their self-concept. The self-concept is "the attributes, abilities, attitudes and values that they believe define them."[3] For example, children develop a self-concept by the age of three and can categorize themselves into things: "I'm a boy"; "I like race cars"; "I like dresses"; "I have blue eyes," etc. As we age, our self-concepts become more complex and deeply rooted. At the core, our self-concept answers the question, "Who am I?"[4]

As your mentee begins a relationship with Jesus, that's the same question they face in their spiritual walk: "Who am I?" Before their walk with Christ, their self-concept was misguided. It was not their true self. Our true self-concept is found only in Christ. Before I came to Christ, and even in the first few years of my relationship with Christ, my self-concept was "I am broken." I felt like there was something wrong with me and I would always be incomplete. This self-concept impacted me spiritually and emotionally.

Scripture tells us that when we receive Christ, we become a new creation. 2 Corinthians 5:17 says, "Therefore, if anyone is in Christ, the new creation has come: The old has gone, the new is here." As followers of Christ, we are reborn into a new identity as sons and daughters of God[5]. The new identity we partake in challenges our previous self-concept and redefines us. Scripture tells us that our new self-concept is a child of God,[6] a saint,[7] an ambassador of Christ,[8] a co-laborer,[9] righteous,[10] new,[11] forgiven,[12] and a temple of the Holy Spirit.[13] As you meet with your mentee, help them align their self-concept to who God says they are. Learning to identify ourselves as what the Lord calls us is a beautiful, but lengthy process. Walk with your disciple through this season of identifying with Christ.

At this stage, your mentee may also start to identify with *you*. They put more stake in your successes and failures; they long for you to succeed and want to be a part of your life. I think of the identification process similarly to becoming an honorary family member. They care for you deeply and vice versa. This is a beautiful image of the fellowship and love between believers. Cherish these moments because it is an incredible opportunity to speak life into your mentee. Examples of these kinds of connections are seen in Paul's writing to Timothy[14] and to the churches of Thessalonica[15] and Galatia.[16] Embrace this closeness to your disciple as you welcome them into your spiritual family.

Stage Three: Exhortation—Adolescence

As your mentee learns their true identity in Christ, they will continue to grow in Him, and their roles and expectations will change. Just as a child develops, they have more responsibilities to take care of themselves, your mentee will be expected to carry a larger role in their own personal and spiritual well-being. As their mentor, it is important that you allow them to experience the weight of this new responsibility so they may mature in the faith. Your disciple needs to be pushed to try and experience new things and grow in different areas. Your mentoring job is to encourage them to be the best version of themselves—even if they don't like it.

The easiest way to describe the relationship between the disciple and discipler in this stage is that of a player-coach model. A coach's job is to push the players outside of their comfort zones to get stronger. As a baseball coach, I constantly push my players to do conditioning workouts. They dread conditioning, but I continue to do it because it helps them become better baseball players.

Push your disciple outside of their comfort zone so they can grow. This will look different for each person you disciple. For some this may mean getting involved in a ministry leadership position. For others, it may be encouraging them to make a new friend with whom to share Jesus. How your disciple needs to develop is based on what you and your disciple agree is best for them.

Paul pushes Timothy by charging him with the role of appointing elders in the church of Ephesus. Timothy was younger than the elders he was appointing, and it appears he was nervous about it. In 1 Timothy 4, Paul encourages Timothy to not look down on himself for his young age.[17] Paul places Timothy in a leadership position and gives him a challenging task not only because it was needed, but because it was an opportunity for Timothy to grow. In this developmental stage, find intentional ways to push your disciple outside of their comfort zone so they can reach their full potential.

Stage Four: Participation—Adulthood

In the fall of 2020, my brother left for his freshman year of college. We are six years apart, and growing up I always wanted to be his role model. I remember coaching his soccer team and teaching him how to drive when he was 12. For so long I got to be that role model for him, and I loved it! We were so close, and he listened to everything I said. But as he grew up, our relationship began to change. He no longer needed me to be his role model, and he didn't listen to my advice anymore. Our relationship had shifted from mentor-student to brothers. Equals.

In a Christian book on the modern-day home, the Balswicks say this about raising children: "God's ideal is that children mature to the point where they and their parents empower each other."[18] The goal is mutuality! My brother and I reached a place of equality, and out of our equality came partnership. He no longer needed me to be anything for him; rather, we simply enjoyed our friendship. We still have deep conversations, but they're open discussions where we're both on the same playing field.

Within your discipling relationships, you'll see your disciples grow up and become spiritually mature adults. As they grow, embrace the changing relationship. Your mindset will shift from a student-teacher to brothers and sisters in Christ who are mutually encouraging one another. When your disciple reaches maturity and you realize that you can no longer adequately disciple them, encourage them to start meeting with someone who is further along in their faith walk than either of you.

I have not felt more honored in a relationship than when my mentor of three years said he had nothing left to teach me. He encouraged me to consider him a friend, and our relationship has deepened because of it. My "new" friend urged me to begin meeting with his mentor, Loren, who is now my mentor, too.

Honor your disciple and recognize their growth in the faith by transitioning from discipler to friend. Paul honors those he works with by referring to them as his partners. In 2 Corinthians 8:23, Paul refers to Titus as his "partner and coworker in your service." The term partner comes from the word *koinonia* which means "that which we share in common."[19] Paul's saying they are in this together. This example shows us what it is like to do ministry with a partner rather than a disciple. Partners have an equal share and voice in the work. As your disciple reaches adulthood, allow them to partner with you equally!

Totally Worth It

Paul's model of discipleship offers an approach that is inclusive to all discipleship relationships. Reviewing the stages, where do you find yourself in the development process? Be honest—it's okay to admit that you are still in the beginning! Part of growing is recognizing where you are starting. Paul's model gives us a tangible way to think about discipleship. Just like a parent, encourage your disciples to grow, develop, and mature to help them become the best version of themselves.

Spiritual parenting can be difficult and messy. You're constantly working through new situations and learning as you go. It's a challenge, but well worth it. There are few moments in life that compare to the joy of seeing someone you've discipled grow up in the faith. I pray you can experience joy like this in your discipleship relationships.

I promise it's worth it!

6

Big Picture Goals

One of my favorite passages in Scripture is Hebrews 12:1-2. This passage tells us to throw off the sin hindering us and fix our eyes on Jesus as we run the race with perseverance God has marked out for us. The idea of "running the race" really resonates with me. Following Jesus can feel like a marathon at times, and it can be challenging to keep trudging along. And sometimes, I've had moments where I've wanted nothing more than to opt out and sit on the sidelines.

One Saturday night, I was ready to throw in the towel. The ministry I worked for helped international students adjust to America, and one of our strategies was furnishing their apartments for free. That Saturday night, I sat exhausted, falling asleep upon a mountain of couches I had to deliver the next morning. My body ached; I was over-caffeinated and underappreciated. All I wanted to do was quit, go home, and sleep. That was neither the first nor the last time I'd felt that way. The only thing that kept me from quitting was keeping my eyes on the prize. God gave me the grace I needed to fix my eyes on Him and press forward.

That same strategy has kept me in the discipleship race when I've wanted nothing more than to quit in faith and discipleship. Just like physical overwork leads to exhaustion, so does mental, emotional, and spiritual overwork. Yes, there have been times I've wanted to give up on mentoring and discipleship, too exhausted by a challenging situation or a difficult attitude—sometimes mine, sometimes theirs, sometimes both—to keep going. Until I get a glimpse of Jesus and remember to look at Him.

I will be the first one to say keeping your eyes on Jesus isn't easy. It's hard. Especially when things are difficult. It is challenging to avoid being distracted by the world. We lose sight of Him and the end goal, and we're prone to swerve off track, running a race not meant for us. Maybe we begin running for money, fame, jobs, political views, or even for a spouse. None of these are bad or evil things; they're just not the prize you're meant to run for.

Unfortunately, running off course is the story of many Christians, both historical and contemporary. They accept Jesus and start running the race. As new believers, they start off strong and have a passion for Jesus. But as time goes on, they lose sight of the goal and drift off course. You can find runners like these in the Old Testament, and the New—Abraham lacked faith, Jacob lied, David abused and had a guy killed to cover it up, Elijah was depressed, and Peter denied he even knew Jesus! You're not alone in the hall of flawed saints.

Most Christians know that becoming more like Jesus is our end goal, but many lack direction for how to get there. Following Jesus can be challenging, and honestly, it's easy to veer off course and lose sight of Christ.

As you meet with your mentee, you become their

"running partner." And it's your job to keep you both on track and focused on the end goal: becoming like Christ. You will find areas to focus and work on along the way. Maybe it's pride, fear, doubt, addiction. Whatever it is, the end goal is the same: becoming more like Christ. Stay on track to reach the finish line.

In this chapter, we'll explore what it means to help your mentee stay on track through the transformation of head, heart, and hands. These areas work like a racecourse's checkpoints to help keep you on track and focused on the finish line.

Big Picture Goals: Transforming the Head, Heart, and Hands[1]

As you run alongside your mentees, they will become more like Christ and their lives will begin to transform. Paul writes, "Therefore, if anyone is in Christ, the new creation has come: The old has gone, the new is here!"[2] We are reborn into a new identity with a new set of purposes. The process of moving from death to life takes time and can be messy, but the whole process breaks down into three areas: heads, hearts, and hands. Take a look at Colossians 3:1–10:

> Since, then, you have been raised with Christ, set your hearts on things above, where Christ is, seated at the right hand of God. Set your minds on things above, not on earthly things. For you died, and your life is now hidden with Christ in God. When Christ, who is your life, appears, then you also will appear with him in glory. Put to death, therefore, whatever belongs to your earthly nature: sexual immorality,

impurity, lust, evil desires and greed, which is idolatry. Because of these, the wrath of God is coming. You used to walk in these ways, in the life you once lived. But now you must also rid yourselves of all such things as these: anger, rage, malice, slander, and filthy language from your lips. Do not lie to each other, since you have taken off your old self with its practices and have put on the new self, which is being renewed in knowledge in the image of its Creator (Colossians 3:1-10).

Notice Paul's separation of the head, heart, and mind. He tells us to set our hearts where Christ is and our minds on things above. He instructs us to rid our hands of the evil things we once practiced. The process of sanctification involves the transformation of these three areas. When you meet with your mentee, keep the transformation of their heart, head, and hands at the forefront of your mind and work to make conversations about these topics an integral part of your time with them.

Head Transformation

Naturally, when we think of the mind, we may think about knowledge. But knowledge is only a part of the transformation of the mind. True transformation is a change in our knowledge, priorities, and understanding of the world.

Transformation of Knowledge

Growing in knowledge of the Lord is essential to maturing in Christ. It is through this knowledge that we grow in our understanding of what Christ has done for us,[3] develop sound doctrine,[4] learn to fight Satan's attacks,[5] and learn to identify false teaching.[6] In 2 Peter 3, Peter shows us the importance of knowledge. He says that we should "be on your guard so that you may not be carried away by the error of the lawless and fall from your secure position. But grow in the grace and knowledge of our Lord and Savior Jesus Christ. To him be glory both now and forever! Amen."[7]

Peter warns the church to be aware of false teachers that skew Paul's teaching[8] and to grow in grace and knowledge of the teaching of Jesus. As a mentor, follow this example by reading Scripture with your mentee. Take opportunities to discuss and teach God's Word and impart biblical truth for the development of your disciple. This is essential to growing in knowledge and the transformation of their mind. If we fail to impart knowledge to our mentee, we run the risk of producing a disciple who does not know the Word. A biblically illiterate disciple is one whose mind is not transformed and is ineffective and unable to share the truths of the gospel.

Big Picture Goals
Transforming the
Head
Heart
Hands

Pursuing knowledge with the young men I mentor often includes impromptu Bible studies. We spend our time together reading a passage of Scripture and then talk about it verse by verse. I love this way of seeking knowledge because it takes the pressure off me to provide crazy wisdom, and it allows the Word of God to speak for itself. Some of the most powerful moments I have experienced with mentees have come from spending time digesting Scripture together.

Transformation of Priorities

Our priorities should shift from seeking the ways of the world to seeking the kingdom of God. In Matthew 6, Jesus tells the crowd, "Do not worry, saying, 'What shall we eat?' or 'What shall we drink?' or 'What shall we wear?' For the pagans run after all these things, and your heavenly Father knows that you need them all. But seek first his kingdom and his righteousness, and all these things will be given to you as well."[9]

Jesus makes it clear that our new priority is to seek the kingdom of God. It is an active choice to put God above money, career, homes, retirement plans, and even family. This is a challenging task. It's easy for Jesus to slip into second, third, or even last place. As a mentor, help your disciple keep their priorities intact by holding them accountable to keep Jesus number one. A transformation of priorities impacts your disciple's willingness to pursue Jesus. A disciple that does not put Jesus first will struggle to take action and become a passive believer.

One of the best mentors I know does a phenomenal job of helping her mentees keep their eyes fixed on Jesus. She has a way of gently reminding the young women she meets with to turn everything back to Jesus. For her, keeping the end goal in mind is as simple as offering gentle nudges to her mentees to stay on track.

Transformation of Worldview

Seeing the world from a God-centered view is essential to living a life pleasing to the Lord. In Romans, Paul says, "Do not conform to the pattern of this world, but be transformed by the renewing of your mind. Then you will be able to test and approve what God's will is—his good, pleasing and perfect will."[10]

As you grow in the knowledge of the Lord, your ability to discern right from wrong will increase, and so will your ability to discern what pleases Him. Notice the way your disciple is making decisions. Are they using discernment? Are they seeing the situation from a God-centered lens or a human lens? Spend time with your disciple processing decisions and seeing what the Lord says about it. The transformation of our discernment is one of the most fruitful conversations I typically have.

Recently I had a discussion with a young man who was having trouble forgiving someone. I asked him what God said about forgiveness, and that simple question launched a discussion about true forgiveness. And we marked out clear action steps he could take to forgive. Exploring what God thinks about things will help us make decisions that are pleasing to God.

The transformation of our heads is essential to growing in the faith. It creates opportunities for you and your disciple to explore God's Word, wrestle with priorities, and see the world through the lens of Scripture. A disciple with a transformed mind is dedicated to God's calling and is equipped to share and defend their faith. Conversations centered on the transformation of our minds are important to our development as believers. But—don't get stuck there! It can be tempting to focus on knowledge over action, but keep in mind how much you are focusing on knowledge. Knowledge without action can lead to complacency, pride, and hinder your ability to be effective for the kingdom. Heart transformation is the only thing that can spur action.

Heart Transformation

Discipleship is rooted in heart transformation. It is only with our hearts that we believe and are justified.[11] Therefore this heart transformation begins with a heart transplant at salvation. Without a transformation of our hearts from stone to flesh everything we do is in vain.

In Ezekiel 36, God says, "I will give you a new heart and put a new spirit in you; I will remove from you your heart of stone and give you a heart of flesh. And I will put my Spirit in you and move you to follow my decrees and be careful to keep my laws."[12]

In the historical context, God is referring to Israel's restitution. In true Israelite (and let's be honest—human) fashion, the Israelites turned away from the Lord, and they were punished. God gives them hope for a time in which they would be fully united to the Lord, a moment wherein true heart transformation would occur, and they would be restored to fellowship with God.

In the larger context, it speaks of God's character and His desire to give all people new hearts. This happens when we accept Christ—we enter into the same redemption God desired and prepared for the Israelites. Through Jesus Christ, we have restored fellowship with God. He has given us a new heart—one that isn't bound to the old sinful ways of thinking and believing, but one that is tuned into the Holy Spirit, ready to follow and fellowship with God.[13]

Of course, the new heart must be healthy to work effectively. A healthy heart is one that abides in Jesus. John 15 shows the metaphor of the vine and the branches. Jesus tells His disciples to "remain in me, as I also remain in you.

No branch can bear fruit by itself; it must remain in the vine. Neither can you bear fruit unless you remain in me."[14]

Our spiritual hearts need to be healthy, finding their purpose and life source in the vine, Jesus. He is our source of life! He is the one who provides for us and gives us the energy to be His followers. Helping your disciple create a healthy heart begins at the source—Jesus. A healthy heart begins and dwells at the feet of Jesus. Spend time helping your disciple abide in Jesus. This can look different depending on the person. It may mean spending time in prayer, reading and studying together, evangelizing, going for a walk in nature, or some other creative activity. Whatever the way, help them make time with Jesus a top priority. When we spend time with Jesus, we begin to care for what He cares for. Our passions, desires, and hearts will start looking more like his. It is out of God's love for us that our hearts will beat in the same rhythm as His.

What breaks your disciple's heart? Is it what breaks Jesus' heart? Does your disciple show compassion for the poor? The adulterer? The addicted? The rebel? The downtrodden? The lost? The seekers? It is out of God's love for us that we are called to love others. In fact, loving as Jesus loves is a sign of salvation.[15]

May our hearts continually be transformed to love others because Christ first loved us.

Help your disciple become aware of any clot in their heart. Just as a clot in your physical heart can cause serious damage, like a heart attack or worse, a clot in our spiritual heart can be devastating. Is there something keeping them from intimacy with the Lord? Are they living in sin? Is there a past hurt they have not gotten over? Help your disciple explore any hindrances to fellowship. Don't be afraid to dig deep and see what's at the heart of the issue. These moments may be challenging for you or may require you to challenge them at times, but that is okay! Their spiritual health—and yours—is more important than your comfort.

Hands Transformation

First things first: the transformation of our hands is not works-based salvation. Scripture is clear that salvation comes by faith alone, and that there is nothing we can do to earn it on our own.[16] Salvation is in Christ alone, through grace alone, by faith alone.

Transformation of our hands, rather, is about our actions being transformed by our relationship with Jesus. In Jesus' ministry on earth, He spent a vast majority of the time equipping His disciples for action—for sharing the gospel and starting the Church. From the beginning, following Jesus meant action, not simply a passive belief or cursory commitment. In fact, the word *disciple* can be both a noun and a verb! Discipleship is something we actively participate in!

In Matthew 25, Jesus tells a parable of three servants who were given different amounts of money (called talents) to use while the master was gone. One servant used his five talents and made five more. Another used two talents and made two more. But the final one hid his talent in the ground. When the master returned and asked for an account of what his servants did with their money, the ones who used and multiplied their gifts were praised. The master says, "'Well done, good and faithful servant. You have been faithful with a few things; I will put you in charge of many things. Come and share your master's happiness!'"[17]

But the one who hid his money was scolded. His master called him a "wicked, lazy servant!"[18] Even worse, the master takes the one talent away from the lazy servant and gives it to the one who already has five. The passage implies that if you do not use your "talents"—whether that's money, skills, time, resources—God may choose to take away the responsibility, or even the talent, and give it to someone else! Whoa.

God has an expectation for us to use what we have been given. It does not matter if you have been blessed with much or little; it matters what you do with it. Notice the master didn't expect the one who was given two talents to produce five, but he was given enough for his specific task.

Keep this in mind as you meet with your mentee; discuss their talents, skills, and resources. Take moments to praise them when they are using their talents and look for opportunities to point out their positive attributes.

As they see their skills, responsibilities, and resources more clearly, encourage them to use their talents for the good of God's kingdom. Encourage your disciple to find opportunities to use their gifts in any context, whether that be in a bakery, account firm, in the home, or in a church. Help them see how they can make a difference today.

Heads, hearts, and hands transformation is at the center of what discipleship is about. These three areas should be the biggest focus of your conversations with your mentee. The examples I've given are not exhaustive, and there are many variations of conversations you can have about your mentee's head, heart, or hands. And you don't necessarily have to frame your conversations with this "transformation" language. But have it in the back of your mind when you interact.

Think of these as a way of grouping conversations as you shape the direction and goal of the conversation. You will find opportunities to explore one of these topics. When you focus on an area worth exploring, dive deep, looking for transformation, not simply exploration. Talking to your mentee about their hardened heart without helping them move toward transformation falls short of our goal. Transformation is a lengthy process. Don't expect it to come in one, two, or even three meetings—it takes time and persistence! Keep working with your mentee until there is evidence of change.

It is also important to note that most conversations with your mentee can cover multiple topics. A single conversation could cover the head, heart, and hands. The three areas are interconnected, and change occurs gradually. Walk through each area as needed and help your mentee recognize that a block in one area impacts how the others operate. For example, if your mentee's heart is hardened against their spouse, their ability to serve them is hindered.

The transformation of the head, heart, and hands is essential to effective discipleship. Without it, we fall short of the goal–becoming like Christ. Keep your eyes on the prize and help your mentee pursue godliness.

Nearly every conversation I have with mentees revolves around these three categories. Why? Because these are the areas that God desires to transform. God desires for our hearts, heads, and hands to be centered on Him. As you meet with your mentee, keep these categories in the forefront of your mind. This is the core of sanctification and what discipleship is all about.

7

The Process of Change

In the previous chapter, you read about the importance of focusing on the heart, head, and hands. As stated, these areas are the foundation of discipleship and the primary focus of discipleship. Of the three areas to focus on, the transformation of the hands, specifically serving, requires the most direct training. For example, if your mentee has a gift for teaching, you may need to spend time training and equipping them with the skills needed to teach.

The model used for the transformation of hands (serving/using giftings) is engage, evaluate, equip, and empower. This model takes you through a step-by-step process of identifying and helping your mentee progress in something specific. This can be accomplished by developing an attribute of Christ or by helping your mentee use their gifts. It's a very hands-on way to think about discipleship, a little more granular in process and ideas, and is a natural outworking of your mentee's ongoing transformation.

In my experience, a helpful way to view yourself in this big picture role is to see yourself as a coach. Your coaching goal is to help your mentee become the best version of himself or herself and produce the best character and fruit possible. I have had a variety of coaches in my athletic career, but the ones that stand out to me are those who took an interest in me as an individual and pushed me to be the best version of myself. Tony Dungy, a hall of fame NFL coach and devout Christian leader, wrote *The Mentor Leader: Secrets to Building People and Teams That Win Consistently*[1] that has influenced my view on leadership development and inspired me to adapt his model to create the engage, evaluate, equip, empower framework. A similar model is used by the Fellowship of Christian Athletes, whose organizational model is identical but does not include the *evaluate* section.[2]

You will cycle through these stages continually with your mentees. Each stage will help you further engage your mentee and lead them on the path to personal and spiritual development.

Engage, Evaluate, Equip, Empower

The first step in this cycle of growth is to engage with your mentee. Take a genuine interest in their life. This requires intentionality. Explore their spiritual life, family, friends, hobbies, coworkers, etc. As you engage, you begin to see them as they truly are. A glimpse into someone's unfiltered life is a true blessing. You see their good and their bad and everything in between. Engaging with your mentee and entering this space is essential to helping them feel known and loved.

I've had the privilege of pouring into a young man named Noah. In the winter of 2019, Noah attended a college ministry retreat that I spoke at, and he gave his life to the Lord. Shortly after the retreat, Noah and I began meeting together. As we developed a relationship, he shared openly about his life, and I had the joy of seeing his life unfiltered. For the next three years, Noah and I met weekly, and he matured rapidly in the faith. He has grown to be a strong and mature follower of Christ.

In the fall of 2021, Noah got a job as a life and family ministry intern at a nearby church, and one of his tasks was to create weekly recap videos for the children's ministry on YouTube. As Noah and I met, I listened as he told me how nervous he was to create the recap videos. I couldn't help but find it funny because he is one of the best communicators I know—Noah could hold a conversation with anyone. And I mean anyone. But he did not recognize his natural talent, and he would not let me watch his videos. But eventually, because of the relational equity I had with him from meeting with him for so long, Noah began sharing his videos with me.

As you engage with your mentee, you will see their life unfiltered. It's a privilege to see someone's life as it truly is. As you get to know them, you will naturally transition into the evaluation stage because you'll likely see areas for growth as you chat. It may be in their maturity, knowledge, actions, or something in between, but they will have room for growth. Evaluation provides opportunities to highlight and celebrate successes, identify areas for growth, and ultimately push them to become more like Christ. The evaluation stage is less of a "grade" and more of an assessment of their positives and negatives.

Take Paul, for example. Paul spent eighteen months with the church of Corinth, building them up in the faith and teaching them the fundamentals of the gospel. After Paul left, he received an update on the church's progress—it wasn't going well. In 1 Corinthians 3:1–4, and on other occasions throughout the letter, Paul gives a not-so-stellar review of the church of Corinth. Based on their actions and behavior, they were misusing Christ's freedom to do terrible things. Paul then spends the rest of the letter addressing errors in the church, giving proper instruction on freedom, and giving instructions for worship. Paul's evaluation directed the rest of his letter to the church.

The Process of Change
Engage
Evaluate
Equip
Empower

So, Noah and I began evaluating his recap videos together. It was uncomfortable for him, but that wasn't surprising. The evaluation stage often is uncomfortable for mentees. After only a few minutes of watching his recap video, Noah had a long list of areas that he needed to grow in.

"Wow, I didn't realize how bad that was," he said and then listed the things he needed to improve.

When it was my turn to share, I gave him my honest assessment: there were areas for growth, but overall he is a good speaker and did a lot of things well. Honest, but encouraging.

As you evaluate your mentee, be sure your evaluation is presented in a way that will be best received by your mentee. An evaluation is only as good as its ability to be received. An evaluation that cannot be received is not helpful. If your mentee responds best to direct feedback, then you need to give a clear evaluation. If your mentee shies away from "the harsh truth," then you must find a way to present your evaluation in a way they can receive it. There will always be room for growth, but there will also always be room for praise.

Please do not skip the evaluation stage, evaluations are important because they are a chance to understand how you can better help your mentee grow. If you never have a dialogue with your mentee about their growth, you hinder their development.

As you evaluate your disciple, reflect on their maturity, decision-making, personal relationships, friendship with God, small group leading skills, speaking skills, etc. Aim to create a broad profile of their strengths and weaknesses.

A word of caution: don't spend too much time evaluating, as you may get stuck in analysis paralysis or worse, overwhelm your mentee.[3] The key is to evaluate enough to find room for growth and then intentionally move into the equipping stage.

The equipping stage is where you spend time with your disciple, actively working on an area of growth. This stage is the broadest of the three stages because each task requires different methods of equipping and different amounts of time.

In the equipping stage, Noah and I spent time looking at foundational teaching skills. He practiced creating messages, making the message applicable to children, and even learned how to add his own personal touch to the message. After a few intentional equipping meetings, Noah had learned the basics and was taking the right steps toward becoming an effective communicator.

The equipping stage is frequently implemented by Jesus and Paul. Jesus uses this stage to invite them into ministry with him. Jesus explains His teachings to the disciples, challenges their understanding of the Word, and gives them chances to use their giftings. Paul's letters to Timothy and Titus have an emphasis on equipping the men to run a church well. Paul gives direction on how to lead a church, how to choose elders, hold firm to the truth of the gospel, and so on. Equipping is essential to maturity.

The final stage in this cycle is the empowering stage. This stage is all about encouraging your disciple to exercise their gifts and talents. Think of the empowering stage as a call to action: "You can, and you are called to do this." The empowerment stage has little to do with learning, but with taking action. You are the coach pushing your player to "get in the game." Think about what's stopping them from taking action. Is it a lack of confidence? Of time? Wrong priorities? Are they having trouble finding a place to use their gifts? Whatever it is, work toward overcoming that obstacle and get them in the game!

One of the most challenging and frustrating things about this stage is that the decision to "get in the game" ultimately rests on your mentee. You may have perfectly equipped them to do something, but they may change their mind and want to do something else, or not do anything at all. As a mentor, it is important that you encourage and sometimes challenge them to use their gifts. A disciple stuck in this stage is one that is equipped but not sent.

Paul empowered Timothy. A young man in a challenging leadership role, Timothy struggled to take hold of the leadership responsibilities given to him. Paul empowers Timothy to do something and to take hold of the leadership God gave him. Paul's empowerment of Timothy put a fire under him to take action. As you mentor others, believe that you have the ability to empower your disciple to do everything God has called them to.

The engage, evaluate, equip, and empower cycle is essential to the growth of our disciples and will help them develop the skills and character needed to succeed.

The next big picture goal we are going to look at is possibly the easiest and most foundational component of mentoring. The big picture goal of making someone feel important is not hard. In essence, it comes down to intentionality and love. As we dive into this big picture goal, think about things that have made you feel important in your life.

The section below serves as an important reminder to us as mentors. Everything above is an important part of discipleship, but is facilitated by a strong and healthy relationship with your mentee. In my personal experience, I've found making my mentee feel important to be one of the strongest catalysts to the development of our relationship. Remember, no one is forcing your mentee to meet with you, so if they don't feel cared for it's unlikely that they will want to keep meeting with you. Make them feel important!

Make Them Feel Important

There's probably someone in your life that fills you up every time you're around them. Maybe it's a sibling or a parent, aunt or uncle, or maybe just a really good friend, a kindred spirit. Whoever it is, there's something special about spending time with that person. We naturally gravitate toward people who make us feel important.

Be that kind of person for your mentee. Create a space for them to feel known and loved. As they feel known, they are able to express themselves freely and process life with you. Simply put, make them feel like they belong.

Twentieth-century American psychologist Abraham Maslow is famous for his theory of human psychological health, known as Maslow's Hierarchy of Needs. In his pyramid of human necessities, Maslow ranked belonging at #3, right after physiological needs (air, water, food, sleep) and safety (secure house, job, health). A sense of belonging is essential for mental and emotional health,[4] but according to an IPSOS Public Affairs study of 20,000 people, 54 percent of Americans say they feel "as though no one knows them well at least sometimes, if not always."[5]

Despite the important need for feeling known, many of us feel we aren't. As a mentor, you have the chance to change this for the people you mentor. You have the opportunity to make your mentee feel like they belong and that someone knows them. Creating a place of belonging is one of your primary roles as a mentor.

When you are intentional with your mentee, they feel important, cared for, and like they belong. Without purpose or intentionality, the relationship may never even get off the ground. From the mentee's point of view, it can be scary getting to know someone new or meeting with someone who wants to invest in them. Sometimes there is a gap that needs to be bridged. Many introductions and first meetings do not go anywhere because of a lack of intentionality. Show intentionality. Set up meetings. Reach out. Be the first one to ask for coffee or lunch. As your relationship progresses, the dynamics will change, and their nerves will settle. I know I've reached a good place with my mentee when they start reaching out, too.

Jesus models for us the importance of intentionality

as He pursued the disciples. Jesus' intentionality with His disciples was countercultural. In Jesus' day and age, disciples were expected to seek out a master and, after careful observation, decide if they wanted to follow that master. But Jesus reversed the role; He pursued them! Jesus did not wait for them to decide. Rather, He chose them, saying, "Come follow me, I will make you fishers of men" (Matt. 4:49). Jesus boldly invites His disciples to accept His offer!

Like Jesus, be bold and invite others to join you. In 2015, Barna research showed that one-third of people are looking for a mentor.[6] Don't be afraid to ask! Take the initiative and invite them to meet. I promise that it's worth it!

Honestly, what this all boils down to is being focused on the end goal: becoming like Christ and loving others well. You don't need crazy formulas or five-step plans for discipleship. Everything in this book is simply a tool to help you on your journey to mentor others. As long as you keep Christ, the true big picture, in mind, you'll be fine! Allow the Holy Spirit to guide you as you lead others to the foot of the cross.

8

A Few Guidelines

Growing up, I loved math.

I loved math because once I understood a new concept or formula, it all made sense. Math, at least basic math, is a matching game between your problem and what formula to use. As long as you know the formulas, you're golden!

Unfortunately, people aren't like math. People aren't simple. There isn't a magic formula that, once discovered, will make someone fall in love with you or make you rich. Life and relationships are just a series of educated guesses as to what we think might work. Our uniqueness is a beautiful thing, but it can make relationships tough—especially discipleship. There isn't a set of formulas or an owner's manual to discipleship; trust me—I've looked. Discipleship, like people, is too unique to have a clear-cut formula or step-by-step process that will handle every situation adequately.

Formulas work for numbers because numbers are consistent. People are not numbers, though. People are different; they have personalities—every personality is different and unique. Every person responds to situations and stimuli differently. Every person has a story of how they got to be who they are. And every person can change depending on the day, the circumstance, even the weather. People are unpredictable.

While people's ability and tendency to constantly change is unpredictable and may be frustrating to you, it's actually one of the most valuable and significant parts of discipleship. The process of discipling is one of constant growth—constantly changing, improving, adapting, developing. Our unpredictable behavior makes discipleship a process we are constantly figuring out. Be willing to embrace the unknown of relationships because that is where real life happens.

So, since people are not numbers, I can't give you a formula for discipleship. But I can give you a couple of guidelines and tips to follow to have success in your relationships. You may think that is contradictory, but there are general rules and tips that we follow in relationships on a daily basis. They don't guarantee success, but they do set you up for it.

Tip #1 Walk Alongside Them

1 Thessalonians 2 models what it means to walk alongside someone in discipleship. Paul walked alongside Thessalonica's church and shared his life intimately with them.

In the passage below, notice the personal language Paul uses as he talks about his commitment to the church when he was with them.

> Just as a nursing mother cares for her children, so we cared for you. Because we loved you so much, we were delighted to share with you not only the gospel

of God but our lives as well . . . For you know that we dealt with each of you as a father deals with his own children, encouraging, comforting, and urging you to live lives worthy of God, who calls you into his kingdom and glory. (1 Thess. 2:7b–8, 2:11–12)

Paul relates his care for them to how a nursing mother cares for her child. Paul didn't have any experience nursing a child, but his analogy shows the depth of the love that he has for the church of Thessalonica. It was a parental kind of love. Think about the attachment between a mother and child: there is utter dependence on the child to receive nourishment from the mother, and the bond is deep. Paul shared his life deeply with the church by working alongside them and teaching in the synagogues. He facilitated a loving relationship by simply being with them.

Paul models for us the companionship that can be fostered between a mentor and mentee. Paul shares life with the church and gives of himself freely to them, and he demonstrates to us the deep love that a mentor can have for his mentee. This kind of intertwining is central to the development of discipleship. Your disciple needs to know that you are there for them and that you have their back. Showing them that you are willing to walk hand-in-hand through the positives and negatives of life will develop a deep and intimate relationship between you and them.

Tip #2: Understand the Relationship

The relationship between a mentor and mentee is unique and unlike any other relationship you are a part of. In discipleship relationships, both the mentor and mentee submit and learn from Christ while the mentee is simultaneously "submitting" to their mentor. Because of the nature of this relationship, it is important that we understand the boundaries and purpose of the relationship.

A) "The Relationship Is One of Equality and Yet Has a Natural Bias."[1] You and your disciple are equals! You are not above them because you are older or know more. You may be considered the wiser of the two or further along in your spiritual journey, but you are still equal. As a mentor, it can be easy to feel like we are above our mentee. It may not be intentional, but it is detrimental. When we allow ourselves to feel superior, we threaten the relationship dynamics. Feeling superior makes us prideful and feel "too good" to reveal our flaws. This may make your mentee hold you higher than they ought and may make them unwilling to share their flaws. In addition, it can patronize your mentee and make them feel less than. Avoid making them feel this way by reminding yourself that Jesus is our measuring stick, not one another. You are both working to be more like Jesus and you both still have a long way to go. Keeping this mindset will help you stay humble and avoid getting a big head.

Although you are equal, there will be a natural bias toward you being the teacher. This natural bias is due to the knowledge that you've accumulated through your life. Because you are further down the road in your spiritual walk, you have the chance to assist your disciple by pulling from the knowledge you have that has worked for you in the past. Think about learning to change the oil for the first time; you relied on your parents, friends, or even YouTube videos to guide you. These people used their knowledge of cars to "disciple" you to be able to do it yourself. You can use your knowledge and experience of God to assist and empower your disciples to grow in faith.

B) Mentoring Is a Collaboration Between You, Your Mentee, and "Everyday Life." You and your mentee are in a constant state of reacting to what life throws at you. You cannot predict what will happen tomorrow; plans change, and you experience new things all the time. As you and your mentee enter a partnership together, you enter into each other's lives. This means that things will come up, plans will change, and you and your mentee will have to figure it out together. I can guarantee you that your relationship with your mentee will never be the way you dreamed it. There will be seasons where it is challenging to meet weekly, there will be moments where you hurt their feelings, and there will even be moments where they avoid you. Whatever happens though it is important that you both mentor and mentee "embrace the unexpected and reduce their resistance to it."[2] This means that instead of arguing, growing disdain for each other, or feeling hurt because they haven't responded, both mentor and mentee need to embrace the unexpected and work to make the relationship work.

However, I want to be clear that not all mentor/mentee relationships will work out. There may become a point at which it is no longer beneficial for you and your mentee to continue to meet. In this case, the discipleship relationship may need to be terminated. Mentors and mentees should discuss the termination of the discipleship process. This does not have to be scary though! I have always been a proponent of the idea that you can support and love someone from close or from afar. If you choose to stop meeting with your mentee you are simply transitioning from cheering them on from close to cheering them on from afar. Do not let the termination of the discipleship process impede your ability to support and love your mentee.

C) "What the Mentee Chooses to Do, Learn, or Ignore from the Mentoring Is Not the mentor's Business."[3] If you are a parent, you know this all too well. You cannot control what your child does. You can try all you like, but ultimately it is up to the child to implement what they have learned. Now it is true that there is a difference between being a parent and a mentor. Parents can discipline their kids easier than a mentor can. As a mentor, it is important to remember your role in the process. Your role is to teach and encourage your disciple to become more like Christ—their role is to live it out. However, as difficult as it may be, whether they choose to fulfill their role though is not up to you. Your disciple may choose to listen to everything you said and then go do the opposite, because ultimately, it's their choice.

As a mentor, I understand how infuriating it can be to not have control of what your mentee does. It hurts to pour into someone and then watch them do exactly what you told them not to. It's hard watching your disciple fail and even harder not to rub it in when the mistake comes back to bite them. As hard as it is, we need to remember that we are not in control of their actions. This is an area that requires patience and an area I need to work on in myself as well. I distinctly remember a moment when I got so mad at one of my mentees that I lost my temper and yelled at him. I told him he was wasting his life and that I was sick of him blaming other people for his failure. I handled the situation poorly, and it damaged my relationship with him as a result. I was so upset with him that he asked to stop meeting with me. At that moment, I realized I had made a huge mistake and had missed an opportunity to effectively mentor this young man.

It is important to note, though, that you should correct your mentee when they make mistakes.

Correcting your mentee is an important aspect of being a mentor and should not be ignored. If your mentee is living in sin, becoming complacent, or making choices that are unhelpful to their relationship with God or their health, you should call them out on it! The mistake I made was believing that I had the right to force my mentee to do what I said, which is not the case at all. Just because you cannot force them doesn't mean that you cannot correct them. To avoid anger or resentment, consider talking to your mentee about your feelings in a loving and corrective way.

Correction

If your mentee is living in sin, becoming complacent, or making choices that are unhelpful to their relationship with God or their health, you should call them out on it!

Following these boundaries will set you and your mentee up to have a healthy relationship. Remember, relationships are messy and both of you will make mistakes, but if you keep the right attitude and healthy boundaries—you will get through it!

Tip #3 Find Your Pace

One of the wisest things I was ever told was by a pastor I meet with periodically named Tom. Tom is one of the sharpest and most knowledgeable men I know, and I am so thankful for his wisdom and influence in my life. During one of our meetings, I was telling him how ministry is so challenging because there is always more to be done. No matter how many men I mentor or how many messages I give, there is always another person who needs Jesus. As I was expressing how disheartening this was, Tom looked at me and said something along the lines of, "There will *always* be more ministry to be done. The key to succeeding is not speed, but pace." The key to success in ministry and mentoring is not to sprint the entire journey, but to find a sustainable pace.[4] Running at a sustainable pace means taking care of yourself and making sure you are being invested in as well. Make sure that you are healthy and growing before taking on new tasks. It is important to note that the pace you can "run" at will change over time and in different seasons of life. There will be moments where you can increase your pace and meet with your mentee more frequently, or even start mentoring someone new. There will also be moments where you need to slow down your pace and meet with your mentee less frequently. As you determine your pace, remember that it ebbs and flows with life. Do not set yourself to one pace forever; allow yourself the freedom to adjust accordingly.

Tip #4 Set Your Boundaries

Although living life with our mentee is the goal, like all relationships, it can get messy if boundaries are not set. Relationships can develop unhealthy tendencies without boundaries and expectations.

Setting healthy boundaries with your mentee is necessary to keep both you and your mentee safe in the relationship. Boundaries act as guardrails on the road to keep you and your mentee on the right track. Without establishing good boundaries, you run the risk of harming your mentee or yourself. In order to set healthy boundaries, you need to determine what is appropriate for your relationship with them. As you consider what are appropriate boundaries for you and your mentee, you need to consider: 1) What are appropriate boundaries to protect me? and 2) What are appropriate boundaries to protect them? These questions may seem drastic, but unfortunately, life gets messy sometimes, and boundaries offer clarity in the mess. As you think about boundaries to protect yourself, you should consider what will protect your emotional, spiritual, physical, and financial wellbeing.

Examples of boundaries that fit in this area are: I do not feel comfortable buying my mentee food when we meet, or I cannot meet with my mentee more than once a week. Thinking about areas that will protect your well-being will help you keep a healthy relationship with your mentee. In addition, consider what will protect your mentee. The easiest way to create boundaries for them is to ask them what boundaries they think are appropriate. Allow them to share honestly about the boundaries they want to set. As their mentor, areas I would encourage you to consider are: Will you allow them to serve in your ministry? How much will you ask them to do? How much influence do you have on their decisions? This area may be more challenging to think about but is essential. Without creating boundaries to protect them and yourself, you can set yourself up for failure.

I have witnessed multiple mentor-mentee relationships waver because boundaries were never set. An example I see, especially in a mentee that is struggling emotionally, is that the mentee reaches out to the mentor too often. The mentor becomes the primary and only source of support and becomes emotionally exhausted. Now you may think setting boundaries is restrictive to the relationship, but it is not. Setting limits on your involvement in your mentee's life actually pushes your mentee to grow. You cannot be their savior or problem solver, it is not healthy, and they need to learn to turn toward Jesus in those moments. Learning to fail and solve problems on their own is an important part of development. Avoid the temptation to swoop in and save them if things are going wrong. In this circumstance, you are the coach and need to allow your "player" to work through it themselves. Knowing when you are too involved or when they are expecting too much from you takes discernment and an assessment of the relationship and your own wellbeing.

I want to be clear here—there will be moments in your relationship with your mentee that are draining or where you feel exhausted. When your mentee is struggling or in a season of loss, confusion, or even discovery, they may need more help. That is okay and you should be there for them in that season. The key is to differentiate between if it is a season or a trend. If it is a season and they need the extra support, then ride it out with them. If it is a trend, then you may need to be more intentional about setting limits on the relationship.

Be cognizant of the boundaries you set with your mentee. Your boundaries are meant for the development of your relationship and their spiritual maturity. Avoid the temptation to be their "savior" and allow them to experience the weight of problem-solving.

Important Note: On the topic of boundaries and mentees who are struggling emotionally, this is important: you are not your mentee's counselor, and you should not try to be.

There are two major problems with this. 1) Counseling is not the goal of discipleship. The goal of discipleship is to become like Christ. 2) Unless you have a professional degree or training in mental health work, you are unqualified to offer mental health counseling. Do not let the desire to be needed or to help cloud your judgment. If your mentee is struggling with serious mental health concerns, they need to see a licensed professional. Please do not be a roadblock to your mentee receiving the help they need.

Tip #5: Share Authentically

If you remember tip #1, you will remember the importance of experiencing life with your mentee. It is essential that we show them that we are there for the highs and the lows. As we live life with them, though, it is important that we share authentically with them about our lives. Transparency develops trust in the relationship and makes your mentee more willing to open up to you.

Research actually shows that mentors who withhold their own faults struggle to develop deep relationships with their mentees.[5][6] A mentor who appears to be perfect can be challenging to open up to[7]. Rather, mentees crave transparency. Regi Campbell says mentees look for these seven characteristics in mentors: authenticity, approachability, emotion, value, believability, a willingness to challenge, and transparency[8]. Sharing authentically is part of developing a genuine relationship with your mentee.

There will inevitably come a time in your conversation with your mentee that they turn the tables on you and ask you how you are doing. This may make mentors uncomfortable; after all, you are supposed to be investing in them. What I am going to tell you may seem unconventional, but it is imperative that when they ask you how you are doing, you answer them authentically. Do not lie and tell them that everything is okay if it is not. Lying or skimming over the questions damages the relationship and makes you seem fake. You may think that sharing takes away from the mentee's time, but it actually enriches it. Showing your mentee that you are not perfect and that you struggle to pursue Jesus at times is important to their development in the faith. Without exposing your flaws, you can unintentionally create a mindset in your mentee that failure is not an option. This can harm their view of grace and make them hesitant to open up to you when they fail. The key to sharing authentically is to share without asking them to explore with you. As you share you want to invite them into your life without asking them to help you figure out what to do. Imagine it as if I showed you a pile of trash. I could say, "Look at all of this trash I have with me," or I could say, "Look at all this trash I have with me. Will you help me sort through it?"

The difference between the two is the expectation placed on the mentee. As a mentor, you need to show your good and your bad, but you cannot ask your mentee to help you sort through it. Be authentic without asking them to explore. This will help your relationship develop but will also avoid placing unrealistic expectations on your mentee. Show them your trash without asking them to sort it with you.

Tip #6: Put Them in Positions to Succeed

As you get to know your disciple, you will see the talents that God has given them. These talents are what make them unique and are an important component of what God is calling them to do (Eph. 2:10, Matt. 25:14–30). Some gifts are apparent and easy to spot, while others may remain hidden. As their mentor, you have the wonderful privilege of helping your disciple see their talents and ultimately use them to bring God glory! As you help them discover their gifts, there will inevitably be opportunities for them to use their gifts.[9]

This is an exciting but precarious situation. It can lead to exceptional growth or decay depending on the outcome. If your mentee is given the right opportunity, they will be encouraged and grow quickly. If they are put in a spot that is either the wrong fit or one that they are unequipped for, they will suffer.

Your mentee needs to be put in the best position to succeed. They need a role that is going to help them utilize their talents and push them to grow. The position needs to be appropriate for their spiritual maturity and should not be too far below or above their aptitude. Choosing an area to serve in which they are underutilized can lead to complacency, while an area above the mentee's skill level can lead to exhaustion. Think of it like you were trying to help your mentee get stronger at the gym. If the weight is too light it will be too easy, and they will not get stronger. If the weight is too heavy, they will be crushed and exhausted. You need to help them find a weight that fits them just right. When we do this, we help them grow in leadership ability and spiritual maturity.

This may come as a surprise to you, but the biggest hindrance to finding the right position is most often the mentor, especially a mentor in a ministerial position.

This error happens when the mentor finds a position for the mentee that benefits the mentor or the mentor's organization. When a mentor has a position for the mentee that also benefits themselves, they may intentionally or unintentionally push it onto the mentee. The mentor needs to remember that the position the mentee chooses needs to be for the mentee's growth, not to fulfill the spot for the mentor. This does not mean that a mentee can never work for a mentor, but it should be done with caution. I've made the mistake of pushing a mentee too hard in a direction I wanted him to go, and it hurt our relationship. I remember him remarking, "I feel like you are always wanting me to do something more." It hurt me to hear because it was true. I was pushing him too hard, and I damaged our relationship. I am so thankful that he has forgiven me for my error and that he still chooses to meet with me.

Allow your mentee to make the final call on decisions and encourage them to choose something that is going to push them to grow! As you help them get into positions to lead, you can help them work through the growing pains of a new position. Continue to be encouraging and help them develop the skills necessary to succeed.

Tip #7: Follow the Flow of the Conversation

As a mentor, show up to every meeting with intention but not with expectations. A mistake you can make as a mentor is to come into meetings with an expectation of how it will go or what you will talk about. You'll be disappointed if you're expecting a life-changing conversation and it doesn't happen. Your plan may actually keep your mentee from sharing what is really on their heart. There is no pressure for anything crazy to happen during your time with your mentee. Sometimes there will be mundane conversations, and other times, transformative conversations.

A Few Guidelines

Rather than coming with an expectation, come with the intention to create a space where life-changing conversations can happen.

Be on the lookout for ways to build your relationship with your mentee, as well as ways to help them grow in their relationship with God. As you talk, look for opportunities to naturally bring God into the conversation. (Keyword: naturally. Don't force it!) There is no formula for discipleship conversations except to be intentional. As you and your disciple meet, you will find a natural flow of conversation that will, hopefully, lead to talking about Jesus. Every relationship will naturally gravitate toward a certain pattern, and that's okay! The pattern may be to read Scripture and talk about it, go through a curriculum, or just talk freely. Whatever it is, own it. The flexibility in the relationship is a wonderful thing! The key here is not the structure but the intention behind it.

Whatever style you and your disciple choose, make it natural! It is common for discipleship relationships to start out structured and transition into more free-flowing conversations. This is because the structure, especially at the beginning, can be a safety net for mentors and mentees. Knowing there is a book or plan can calm nerves. As you grow in comfortability with your mentee, your conversations will likely become more free-flowing, and less structure will be necessary. Whatever style you choose, just be sure to be flexible, natural, and keep the end goal in mind.

Following these tips will not guarantee a perfect relationship or conversations with your mentee, but they will put you in a position to succeed. Walking alongside them creates an atmosphere of vulnerability and intimacy, and keeping healthy boundaries helps protect you and your mentee from developing an unhealthy relationship. Putting your mentee in positions to succeed will help them grow in their faith and utilize their talents, and embracing flexibility in the relationship will make it feel more natural and fun. If you follow these tips, you will create a platform for a healthy and honest relationship with your mentee that can lead to life transformation!

9

The Search Begins

I was an awkward kid. Being awkward as an early teen is not abnormal, but my awkwardness was palpable—especially with strangers. I didn't know how to start conversations and often missed social cues. In the eighth grade after an awkward interaction with a doctor, my mom told me I was acting very weird. In the tenth grade, my dad gave me a forty-minute lecture about the importance of body language in conversations and how I should always try to smile when someone is talking to me. They clearly thought that I was not catching on, and they were right. After one too many embarrassing conversations, I started researching conversational strategies and different listening techniques that would help me have better conversations.

Throughout the years my research has moved from asking the internet questions like, "how do I start a conversation?" to a passion for learning how to listen. Along the way, I have learned some helpful tips. These tips are by no means an exhaustive list; the art of communication is far too broad of a topic to cover in detail here, so we'll take a broad view as it applies to discipleship and mentoring.

First: everyone loves to talk about themselves. Unless you live under a rock, you know this to be true. On average, people spend 30–40 percent of their conversations talking about themselves. This means that 60–80 percent of conversations are with people talking about themselves.[1] This number jumps to 80 percent on social media platforms.[2] Why is this the case, though? Out of all the incredible things in the world to talk about, why talk about ourselves? The answer is because it feels good. Research by the Harvard Institute Social Cognitive and Affective Neuroscience lab has shown that when we talk about ourselves areas in our brain associated with reward and pleasurable feelings light up.[3] We love to talk about ourselves because talking about ourselves is inherently pleasurable. Furthermore, their research shows that we have even higher levels of pleasure when we know someone is listening to us.[4] This means that listening to someone talk about themselves makes them feel good and, ultimately, valued. Listening to others is one of the easiest and surefire ways to make someone feel valued.

> **Listen!**
> Listening to someone talk about themselves makes them feel good and, ultimately, valued.

As a mentor, take the time and energy to really listen to your mentee. I promise it's worth it.

Looking the Part

Listening to your mentee begins with showing them that you are listening. This may seem redundant, but showing someone you are listening is just as important as actually listening to what they are saying. And this boils down to body language. If you seem uninterested, preoccupied, or annoyed, chances are they will stop talking. If you are interested, invested, and present through your body language, you show them they are important and worth your time. Compare the two listening experiences Andy has with his mentors and how their listening impacts his experience.

Andy, a new father in his early thirties, attended a service at his church and, after a convicting message, felt a push to grow deeper in his faith. Andy has been distant from God and his community and has been struggling with transitioning into parenthood. Andy knows he needs help. So he asks his pastor what to do, and he suggests that Andy start meeting with Jim. Jim is an elder in the church, a father of five, and it seems like the perfect fit. The two make plans to get coffee. Andy, a little nervous, gets to the coffee shop a few minutes early and gets a table. Jim arrives five minutes late. As Jim and Andy begin to talk, Andy notices that Jim seems fidgety. He keeps moving the saltshaker back and forth, his leg is bouncing up and down, and after a while, he crosses his arms and leans back. Andy pushes forward and continues to share. About thirty minutes into the conversation, Andy believes Jim has lost interest. Jim's eyes are darting around; he's looking off into the distance, distracted by any other conversation in the coffee shop, and has checked his phone three times. It's clear to Andy that Jim is not interested in what he is saying. When Andy stops sharing, Jim waits a moment, and without commenting on what Andy just said, Jim starts talking about himself and his experience in fatherhood. But his sharing is not fruitful and does not address any of the things Andy talked about. As the time ends, Andy leaves discouraged and feels worse than when he started.

Jim's behavior screamed, "I am not interested in you, and I do not have time for this!" He did a terrible job showing Andy that he was interested and hurt the relationship as a result. You may think Jim's behavior is an extreme example, but it's not. I've seen far more egregious examples of this in my time in ministry.

If you don't show your mentee that you are listening, you'll have trouble developing a good relationship with their mentee.

Let's revisit this story again, but contrast Jim's listening style with Daryl, Jim's replacement.

Discouraged from meeting with Jim, Andy went back to the pastor for another recommendation. Daryl, an elder in the church and a father of two, again seems like the perfect fit. The two make plans to get coffee. Andy, a little nervous, gets to the coffee shop a few minutes early and gets a table. Daryl walks in right on time. Daryl asks Andy to share his story and what he is going through. Andy begins to share, and although still nervous from what happened last time, he opens up. Daryl is facing Andy, making good eye contact, following along with the conversation, and adding small affirmations as Andy shares. In the middle of the conversation, Daryl's phone buzzes, and he apologizes and puts his phone face down on the table. Andy continues to share and feels comfortable going deeper. Daryl asks Andy questions and actively seeks to understand what Andy is saying. Daryl listens empathetically, offers comfort, and then shares briefly about his experience as a dad and relates it back to Andy's story. From there, Daryl leads Andy through a few passages of Scripture on being a father and trusting God. The conversation continues, and it helps Andy identify areas of growth and relieve his anxiety. They plan to meet again, and this time, Andy drives away feeling much better and thankful that he has found someone who understands him.

Andy's response and comfort varied greatly between his interactions with Jim and Daryl. Jim, a primarily passive listener, seemed uninterested in what Andy was saying and did not engage in the conversation. Daryl, on the other hand, actively listened to Andy and showed Andy that he cared about him. Daryl demonstrated what it looks like to show you are listening.

Below is a list of attributes taken from the field of counseling[5] that shows someone that you are listening. As you read this list, take a moment for self-assessment. Ask yourself how many of these attributes/skills you use while you are in conversation.

> *Eye Contact:* Keep eye contact when they are talking. It shows them that they have your attention. Don't be weird about it—you're not having a staring contest!
> *Facial Expressions:* Try and match the person's facial expressions. If they are sad, have an empathetic face. If they're happy, smile with them.
> *Smiling:* Smiling shows that you support them and enjoy their company.
> *Head Nods:* When they are making a point, use head nods to affirm what they are saying or that you understand.
> *Body posture:* Ask yourself if your body posture shows you're giving them your full attention. If you are turned away or hunched, you probably look uninterested.
> *Affirmation:* the use of "yeah," "uh huh," or other

small phrases like this can show them you are listening. But be careful not to use these when your disciple shares something negative.

Tone of voice: Match their tone of voice. If they are sad, be sad with them. If they are excited, match their energy.

Encourage them to keep talking: If you sense they are wrapping up a point but there is more to be unpacked, encourage them to keep sharing.

Avoid distractions: put away things that are going to distract you from the conversation. Your goal is to be completely there for the client. Turn your phone on silent!

Avoid interruptions: Generally, avoid interrupting them. Allowing them to share fully helps them feel comfortable to share more vulnerably. Sometimes interruptions are okay if the person is rambling. In those moments, interruptions are helpful to get the conversations back on point.[6]

Following these guidelines will transform your conversations. They set the foundation for good listening skills and will help make your disciple feel cared for. I taught a small group of men these skills and you would not believe the impact it made on the quality of conversations they began having. Even though they knew we were practicing these skills, they were more willing to share with each other and said they felt more supported by the other men in the group.

Take another moment to review the list. You may notice that none of the skills are particularly difficult; they just take intentionality. You already know how to do a majority of these skills; you just need to learn to implement them in your conversations with your mentee. They don't guarantee success, but they do show your mentee that you are listening.

Now that you learned how to *look* the part, how do you actually *act* the part?

At this point, you know how to look like you are listening, but *looking* like you are listening and *actually listening* are two very different things. Our goal in listening is trying to understand the message your mentee is trying to communicate.[7] As we talk about listening, it may be helpful if we break listening down into two levels: general listening and meaningful listening.

General listening is listening that understands the content and surface feelings of what your mentee is saying. This type of listening gains comprehension of what is being said, but may miss the deeper meaning of what the mentee is saying. Understanding the content simply means comprehending what your mentee is saying. For example, your mentee says, "I am so frustrated with my kids. I feel like they never respect my decisions." You understand they are frustrated with their children's disrespect. Understanding content is typical in everyday conversation. Understanding how your mentee is feeling or what they are really saying is a slightly more challenging task. Your mentee may not always verbally express their feelings, so you may need to infer how they are feeling based on their words and nonverbal actions. For example, if your mentee is talking loudly or seems tense, they may be angry. This is generally an easy task if your mentee is expressive, but if they are stoic, it may require more discernment.

Meaningful listening aims to understand what your

mentee is truly saying. This style of listening looks beyond your mentee's words and searches for a deeper meaning. Learning to identify the meaning behind what someone is saying takes time and is a developed skill. Behind your mentee's words are hidden clues that point to something deeper. It is like a couple arguing over how to fold towels. Most of the time, the fight is not actually about the towels, but mutual respect or understanding. The goal of listening is to try to understand what our mentee really means, not just what they say.[8]

As you think about general listening and meaningful listening, it is important to understand the end goal of listening—to further the conversation. Your goal in listening is engaging with your mentee. Find topics you can explore further with them. As you listen to your mentee, sift through what they are saying to determine what is worth exploring and what can be put aside. Your goal is to find the content that is worth holding onto.

As you listen, ask yourself these kinds of questions:

1. What are they trying to say?
2. What do they seem to be most focused on?
3. What is the "SparkNotes" version of what they are saying?
4. Who is the main character of their story?
5. How are they feeling?
6. What are they really saying?
7. Is there a deeper meaning to this story?
8. What emotion do they seem to be conveying?
9. What nonverbal behaviors are they exhibiting?
10. How are they actually feeling?

So now you know how to look like you're listening and how to listen. Good! These are your bread-and-butter skills and will be used in every conversation.

At this point, you may be thinking, "We've talked a lot about the goals of discipleship, boundaries to set, and even learning how to listen, but how do I disciple someone? How do I have a conversation about Jesus with them?" Here is where we are going to explore that. I truly believe that within every conversation, there is an opportunity for life change! We just need to know how to facilitate it. Throughout the rest of the book, I will use the analogy of a treasure hunt. Imagine with me that finding a conversation centered around God is like searching for buried treasure in a field. The treasure chest is full of gold, but the only problem is that you don't know where it is. Searching for the treasure takes time and effort, but it's well worth it. In your conversations with your mentee, there is a chance to find treasure in every interaction—you just have to search a bit. In the section below, we will look at different types of conversations and how to go from small talk to life change.

Everyday Conversations to Life Change

I hate small talk. It drives me crazy! I couldn't care less about the weather or last night's sports scores. I just want to have deep conversations from the get-go. Small talk always seemed pointless to me when I could be talking about Jesus. When I first started mentoring, I avoided small talk like the plague. I did everything I could to get from "Hi, my name is Kyle" to "Tell me your life story" as fast as possible. A few months into mentoring a couple of young men, one of my friends pulled me aside and told me that

I was being weird and kind of intense. I was making people feel uncomfortable because I was jumping into deep topics without building relationships first. I thought she was being dramatic and that no one could be thinking that until I brought the conversation up to my mentor. To my dismay, he confirmed that I was, in fact, being weird and that my intensity was making people uncomfortable. It was at that moment that I realized I had to bite the bullet and learn the art of small talk.

At first, I was horrible at it. Like, really bad! It felt awkward, and I never felt like I had anything to talk about. I struggled to find conversations that lasted and often jumped back into deeper topics because this type of interaction was so out of my comfort zone. As I stuck with it, though, I realized that small talk is essential to building relationships! Talking about common interests like TV shows, sports teams, cooking, video games, or books can make people feel safe and helps build a stronger relationship with the other person. Having something in common with your mentees gives you a kind of failsafe if conversations go awry or if you do not know what to talk about. Use your common interests to learn more about each other. A good friend who has been working in human resource development for forty years has found that the greatest predictor of mentoring relationships success is if they can bond over common interests. Talking about fun, silly, and light things help keep the time you have together enjoyable.

Small talk is a natural and wonderful part of our lives and our discipleship relationships. You will start nearly every conversation with your disciple in small talk, so embrace it! It is important for the development of your relationship. Allow yourself the freedom to enjoy talking about whatever comes up.

But the key to small talk is learning how to navigate from small talk to in-depth conversations.

Navigating from Small Talk to Life Change

You may feel like the transition from talking about sports and the weather to Jesus seems daunting. Connecting the two may seem lightyears away, and the journey unclear. This gap may scare you, but I promise it's not as treacherous as it seems. The journey from small talk to life change only requires intentionality and a little bit of curiosity.

Dr. Gary Smalley developed a model that encompasses the different types of conversations that happen in marriage.[9] Although marriage is different from mentoring, his teaching can be beneficial for all of us. Dr. Smalley breaks conversations down into six levels, moving from the least intimate to the most intimate. The levels he uses are small talk/cliques, sharing facts, opinions, feelings, needs, and beliefs. There is value in exploring each level, but for simplicity's sake, we are going to simplify these levels into four areas: small talk, general conversation (sharing facts and superficial opinions), meaningful conversations (sharing feelings and true opinions) and life-changing conversations (sharing and exploring beliefs). The further we get down the ladder, the more intimate and meaningful the conversation becomes and the better chance you have of finding treasure. As we look at each level, think about where you and your mentee's conversations land and how you can dive deeper.

Small talk: These are the kind of conversations that

rely on superficial statements ranging from "nice weather we're having" to sharing facts about yourself like "I work at the office down the street." Small talk can also include sharing facts or head knowledge: "Did you see the Lions won last night?"[10] Small talk is an important part of conversations and helps set a positive atmosphere but does not lead to life change.

General conversations are where we spend the majority of our time. General conversations revolve around sharing facts about ourselves, our mutual interests, and offering our opinions. These kinds of conversations can be thought of as a conversation with a friend. These are important, but without additional effort, the conversation will fizzle out or remain at the same depth. Don't skip these conversations—they're important to developing a friendship and help keep the relationship from becoming too serious. Use these moments to talk about what's been going on in their life and casually catch up. Pay attention in general conversations because they are the most likely to produce something worth exploring.

Meaningful conversations are essential for healthy mentor-mentee relationships. One of your primary roles is to be a person your mentee can confide in. This stage requires intentionality and effort. Meaningful conversations are the "how are you really doing?" or "how are you and your mother doing?" kinds of questions. Dive deep, and intentionally listen to what they say about their life. Meaningful conversations focus on sharing opinions, feelings, and needs. It is a place for your mentee to be vulnerable and open. Give your mentee your full attention as this level of conversation—it's where things get real. It is in meaningful conversations that you are most likely going to find something worth exploring. Don't miss this opportunity by bouncing back up to general conversations. Stay here with them!

Meaningful conversations are where I most often find mentors and mentees getting stuck. Mentors do a great job intentionally catching up and hearing about the lives of their mentees, but then are unsure of the next steps to dive deeper. Our mentoring goal is to help our mentees grow in their relationship with Jesus. It is essential to get to a place with them where we can have life-changing conversations. This requires a mentality shift. Life-changing conversations have to be our goal. If you are okay just catching up, I encourage you to reconsider. Jesus is far too important to stop our conversations before life changes.

If you feel like you're stuck in meaningful conversations, never moving to life-change conversations, I want you to know that it's okay for a period of time. You are already doing a great job of being a safe space for them to share. But don't get stuck there. We need to take it one step further. Diving deeper just takes a mindset change, and a little bit more effort. Digging deeper is as simple as knowing its importance, and having a few special "digging tools." These tools don't require a lot of skill to use—just a bit of intentionality.

The two biggest tools that we can use to get beyond meaningful conversations and into life change are attention and intention[11]. All life-changing conversations between a mentee and mentor are a result of the right intentions with the right attention. In conversations, we often do not have a clear aim for the conversation. Conversations with spouses, friends, or family members are usually free flowing, without direction. But when you meet with your mentee, you need direction because it's a meeting with a purpose: to help them know God. You must keep this intention in mind to keep you and your disciple pointed toward Christ. If you lose sight of this goal, you'll lose traction with your disciples, and the relationship will fizzle out into monthly "hangouts." Having good intentions and keeping the right mindset helps us stay on course in our relationships and push our disciples to know Christ.

Having good attention is as simple as a shift in priorities. The attention you give someone matters. Just think about times in your life when someone has not given you their full attention. It hurts. When you are with your mentee—or anyone, for that matter—it's important you give them your full attention. This means you must rid yourself of distractions, clear your mind, and be fully invested in what your mentee is saying. Paying attention helps you ask questions, discover their opinions, feelings, or beliefs on a topic, and make them feel cared for.

If you use these tools, which are really just a mindset, you'll be able to move beyond meaningful conversations and into life-changing conversations. Keep your intention and attention at the ready. In the next chapter, you'll need your detective hat and a bit of curiosity to find the treasure, so be ready!

10

Finding Your X

One of my favorite TV shows is a mid-to-late 2000s mystery/comedy series called *Psych*. Shawn Spencer, the lead character, and his partner, Burton Guster, otherwise known as Gus, work together as criminal consultants for the Santa Barbara police department, using Shawn's "psychic" powers to solve crimes. The only problem that Shawn and Gus have is that Shawn does not actually have psychic powers—just incredible observational skills as a result of Shawn's dad, who trained Shawn to be hypervigilant and inquisitive. Shawn's observational skills made him an incredible detective as he routinely solves cases that have gone cold.

I love this show for a lot of reasons, but what I love most is that it is just out of the grasp of reality. Shawn's observational talent is just barely a superpower. He could read full sentences on someone's paper across the room, notice the direction that the carpet was facing, and see the smallest piece of glass at the scene of a crime. He was truly superhuman, but not superhuman enough to seem unattainable. He could not fly, lift heavy things, or turn invisible, his only superpower was his ability to observe. There is still some part of me that believes if someone spent enough time and effort to perfect their observational skills, they could be like Shawn.

Although we may never reach Shawn Spencer's level of noticing, I believe that there is something that we can learn from him—noticing is the key to discovery. Shawn's ability to notice the small things and explore them is what makes him a great detective. In our relationships with our mentees, we can dive deeper into our conversations by noticing "clues" to explore further. As we wear our detective hats as we talk with our mentees, we will find topics that will lead to life-changing conversations.

Finding Your X

Every conversation has a treasure to be found. Every conversation can lead to life change because God has a say in everything! In every conversation, we disclose our worldviews, self-concepts, thoughts, feelings, beliefs, and actions. Within every one of these topics, God has something to say! Life-changing conversations can happen in any, and I mean *any*, conversation.

In the last chapter, we talked about four different types of conversations: superficial, general, meaningful, and life-changing. Each type of conversation is important to the development of the relationship, but only one leads to transformation, life-changing conversations. Getting to a life-changing conversation may seem daunting at first, but it does not have to be. The key to getting to these kinds of conversations is to look for clues and hints to dive deeper. Hidden within our general and meaningful conversations are clues that, if you notice and explore, will lead to life-changing conversations.

You may not believe me that there are clues to be found, but I promise there are. As people talk about themselves, they give you valuable information about themselves and what they think about the world. As they talk, their intentions, thoughts, feelings, beliefs, and worldviews seep out of their words. Your role as a detective is to use this knowledge to find a topic to explore further. This detective skill is actually similar to the skills counselors use to help their clients explore areas in their life. One of the places you are most likely to find clues is in the stories your mentees tell you. Stories are one of the primary ways we share life with one another. Through stories, we communicate what we believe to be true, what we believe about the world, what we are experiencing, and how we respond to different situations. When you meet with your disciple, you are bound to hear stories about their life. You may hear about their family, friends, relationships, ministries, and everything in between. In these stories, you will find the clues needed to dive deeper.

The type of clues that you are looking for reveals something about your mentee's feelings, thoughts, actions, or beliefs that could lead to a conversation about Jesus and what he calls us to.

As you listen to the story, you can ask yourself these kinds of questions to search for clues:

What is the purpose of their story? Are they telling a joke? Are they trying to process something that happened? Are they exploring a topic they have not had the chance to talk about yet? By understanding the purpose of the story, you can use this to gain clarity on if the conversation can lead to something fruitful. If not, keep looking for other clues.

Is there something that could be explored further? Did they share something that could be fleshed out further, or was not very clear? If so, consider asking them to tell you more about it.

Is there a chance for them to grow from it? If there is a chance for growth, explore the topic further to help them grow in emotional and spiritual maturity.

How does this relate to their past? How does the story they are telling relate to other things they've told you?

Does it line up with the truth? Did they say something that is not an accurate understanding of God's word? This is a great area to explore further to develop an accurate understanding of God's Word.

What does God say about the situation? Is what they are saying consistent with Scripture?

Can I praise them for something they did? Be willing to praise your mentee when they do well. They need encouragement!

How are they feeling? Do they seem excited, angry, sad, contemplative? Based on how they feel, you know what needs to be explored or celebrated.

What is the most important part of what they are saying? Use this clue to help you decide what part of the story you want to focus on. Do you need to focus on what they are thinking, feeling, or what they are doing?

Is there an opportunity for them to use their gifts? Could they better use their talents? Do they need to be encouraged to get involved? Use this clue to start a conversation on taking action. [12]

Another more subtle clue that you can pick up on the

most important point is the tone of their voice and their body language. If they are cautious about what they are saying—slow and thoughtful, sad or avoidant—it may be something that they are having trouble dealing with and would benefit from talking about. If they are excited about something, it may be something worth celebrating with them.

As we cycle through these questions and listen, they will help us discover clues to explore further. By noticing clues, we could take the conversation from meaningful to life-changing. Exploring room for growth is unique to the mentoring relationship. It is unlikely that your mentee's friends or family are actively looking to push them to grow. You have the unique opportunity to actively look for room for growth or praise in your disciple's life. Take hold of that responsibility

It is important to note that not everything your mentee says is going to be full of good conversation material. In fact, most of it will not. If nothing is sticking out to you as you are listening, do not force the conversation. Continue in general and meaningful conversations until you find something else worth exploring. Additionally, there will be times when you find a clue, and it does not lead you to a life-changing conversation. When this happens, just circle back to general and meaningful conversations and try again with a different topic.

Finding conversations to explore is challenging and takes time. Do not be discouraged if you cannot find a topic. The key is that when you find a topic, you stick with it.

As you wear your detective hat and think about areas you can explore with your disciple, there may come a time when you are not sure what to ask. Consider using these tools to help you find a topic worth exploring.

Walk a Mile in Their Shoes

A tool that will assist you on your quest to find clues and the right question to ask is understanding. Now, I'll be honest; I'm not usually a fan of cliché sayings—I often think that they are overused or untrue. But in this case, I believe that "walking a mile in their shoes" is a good cliché that will help us understand where our mentee is coming from.

Understanding your mentee's perspective will help you to find something to explore with them. Without truly understanding what they are thinking or feeling, you will have trouble asking questions and aiding them. Walking a mile in their shoes helps you develop empathy for them, understand why they are thinking the way they are, and keeps you from saying something foolish. There is nothing worse than being given advice from someone who does not know the situation or what you are going through. Throughout my life, countless people have tried to tell me how to get over depression without ever getting to know my story. Their shallow advice left me feeling more alone than when I began, and I made sure not to tell them my true feelings again. Offering advice without seeking understanding can lead to resentment, frustration, and ultimately, a fizzling out of the relationship.

Walking a mile in someone's shoes is not challenging, but it can be time-consuming. Understanding someone's perspective requires time. It takes time to get to know someone's story and why they are the way they are. Understanding your mentee's perspective will become easier as your relationship develops. To understand your mentee's perspective, consider: *what they are saying, what they have said to you, where they are in life, what they believe about themselves, and where they are in their spiritual journey.* Understanding these areas will help you understand why they think, feel, or act a certain way and lead to life-changing conversations.

What They're Saying

If you listen carefully to what people are saying, you may be able to piece out the reason why something is happening. When we speak, we give a rationale for thoughts, feelings, and actions. We justify our behavior, and build arguments that support what we did. This is a moment for mentors to note the reasons they give. If the person you are meeting with says that they are scared to lead a small group because they feel ill-equipped, too immature, or don't have time, you gain insight into why they are saying no. Understanding their perspective helps you navigate the conversation and discuss the barriers stopping them from leading. If you do not understand why they are hesitant to lead, your time with them may be unfruitful. Understanding the reasons they are giving is essential to offering good counsel. Jesus is a master at using what others are saying to lead to life-changing conversations. In Luke 7:36–50, Jesus is eating at Simon's house. As Jesus was reclining, a woman came to him and anointed his feet with oil. Simon, a Pharisee, began to judge Jesus in his mind saying to himself, "If this man were a prophet, He would know who this is and what kind of woman is touching Him—for she is a sinner" (Luke 7:39b). Jesus, knowing what Simon is thinking, uses this as an opportunity to teach Simon about grace. Jesus responds by saying:

"Simon, I have something to tell you."

"Tell me, Teacher," he said.

"Two men were debtors to a certain moneylender. One owed him five hundred *denarii*, and the other fifty. When they were unable to repay him, he forgave both. Which one, then, will love him more?"

"I suppose the one who was forgiven more," Simon replied.

"You have judged correctly," Jesus said.

Jesus uses what Simon said as an opportunity to correct Simon's view of grace. Like Jesus, we can use what our mentee says to help them reach a greater understanding of the faith.

What They Have Said or Done in the Past

In addition to understanding what they are saying, you can think about what they have done or said in the past. Think back to what they have said and how their past experiences influence them today. Does what they are saying now relate to something they talked about in the past? For example, if David said that his ex-girlfriend cheated on him in the past, he may have harbored anger toward her that needs to be addressed. Or, if David is falling out of his church community and has struggled to stay connected in the past, you could confront him on the issue. Understanding our mentee's past is essential to understanding who they are and why they do what they do. As you understand their past, you can use that information to understand the present and use that knowledge to encourage, teach, or challenge them. An example of looking at the past is seen in Paul's confrontation with Peter in Galatians 2. In this passage, Paul uses his knowledge of Peter's previous actions, eating with the Gentiles, as a means to challenge Peter's desire to be a people pleaser. This is a good example of using previous events to add context to a present situation. Look for opportunities to use what your mentee has said or done in the past to help them become more like Jesus.

Where They Are in Life

Understanding what stage of life your mentee is in will help you understand what they are going through. Everyone goes through developmental stages in their life: getting married, having kids, or becoming an empty nester, to name a few. Understanding the stage of life your mentee is in will help you assist them. Think about the common stressors for a person that age and how they might be feeling. A college student may be worried about their life purpose and be looking for direction, while a fifty-something man may be struggling with life regret. By knowing the stage of life they are in, you can help offer better support and guidance to help them navigate that season better. A biblical example of this is seen in Paul's letter to Timothy. Timothy was a young man serving as a leader in the Church of Ephesus. In 1 Timothy 4:12, Paul acknowledges Timothy's youth and encourages him to be the leader God has called him to be "Don't let anyone look down on you because you are young, but set an example for the believers in speech, in conduct, in love, in faith and in purity." Paul's advice is written out of an understanding of some of the specific struggles Timothy would be experiencing as a young leader. This age-specific advice may have eased

Timothy's nerves and helped him become a better leader. Like Paul, be sensitive to where your mentee is in their life to understand where they are coming from and how you can assist them.

What They Believe About Themselves

Understanding what your mentee believes about themselves helps you get to the core of who they are. What we believe about ourselves impacts everything we do, say, and think. Ask yourself, "what does the voice inside their head say?" That voice may be self-critical, distrusting of others, prideful, or best-case scenario, healthy. Whatever is at the center of a person's core beliefs is going to significantly affect the way that person sees and interacts with the world and God. For example, if Sarah has low self-esteem, she may be unwilling to accept the compliments that you are giving her. Understanding a person's self-concept is the most challenging of these tasks, but when you truly understand them, you can challenge and love them in a whole new way. One of my favorite examples of using what your mentee believes about themselves is Jesus' reunion with Peter after Jesus' resurrection (see John 21). After Peter's denial and Jesus' crucifixion and resurrection, Jesus appears to the disciples while they are fishing. When Peter realizes it is Jesus, he jumps into the water to swim to him. This is the first time Peter has spoken to Jesus since his denial, and I can imagine the shame Peter must have been feeling. In a beautiful conversation between Peter and Jesus, which is too detailed to unpack fully here, Jesus helps Peter move beyond shame and into a deeper relationship with God by meeting Peter where he is. Take note of what your mentee says about themselves and work toward correcting their view of themselves to what God says about them.

Where They Are in Their Spiritual Journey

The last area, and the most important area, that will help you find a topic worth discussing, is where your mentee is on their spiritual journey.

Your mentee's spiritual health and maturity is your number one priority. Their maturity in the faith will dictate a lot of how they see and interact with the world. If they are young in their faith, they may need help understanding the fundamental truths of Christianity or what God's role in their life is, while more spiritually mature Christians may need help acting out their faith. Understanding where your mentee is in their spiritual walk takes time, but as you talk with them try to notice how God fits in their life. This may lead to conversations that are focused on the transformation of their hands, heart, or head.

Jim Putman, in his book *Real Life Discipleship*, does a

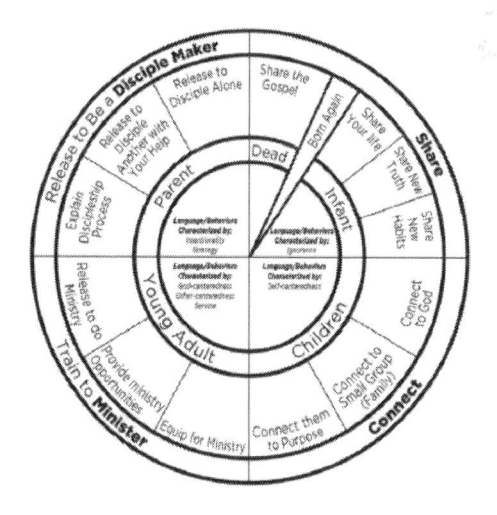

good job breaking down the different stages of the spiritual walk and what a disciple needs from a mentor in each stage. Below is an overview of the discipleship model that Jim created.[13] I believe there is a lot to learn from this model; make sure to look at it carefully![14]

This wheel represents the different needs of a mentee in their spiritual journey. This process is broken down into four steps: share, connect, minister, and disciple.

Share: At the beginning of a mentee's faith, it is the mentor's role to intentionally share the truths of the gospel with our mentees. We need to look for opportunities to share the Word and our lives with them. As you do, you will help them develop a strong foundation built on the Word.

Connect: As your mentee matures in their faith, your role is to help them connect to God, others, and the Church. In this stage, you need to emphasize the importance of relationships and community. Learning to connect and be a part of the body of Christ is an important component of the faith. Look for opportunities to discuss community and the church's role in believers' lives.

Minister: As your disciple is growing and becoming a mature believer, they should use their gifts and abilities to glorify the Lord. In this stage, you are focused on the transformation of your disciple's hands. Look for opportunities for them to use their gifts and encourage them to take leaps of faith. Mentors in this stage should focus on equipping their disciples to act and encouraging them to serve.

Disciple: Your disciple has become a mature believer and is in the process of learning to disciple others. As a mentor, your role is to encourage your disciple to take action and empower them to mentor others. As you and your mentee reach this stage, your relationship with them changes—you transition from mentor to friend. Embrace this change and use it as a chance to edify your mentee.

I hope that you take the time to commit these four steps to memory. They are useful and will help you decide what way you want to take the conversation and how you should approach it.

Noticing clues is not hard; you can do this! With the right intention and attention, you could dive deep with your disciple and break the barrier of general and meaningful conversation to get to life-changing conversations. Be patient with yourself as you practice. Noticing things takes time, and you will get better at it with practice. The key is to keep your eyes focused on pushing your disciple toward Jesus.

When You Cannot Find Treasure, Bring Your Own

I have some bad news for you. No matter how good you get at having conversations and noticing chances to dive deeper, there are going to be times when you will not find something to explore. It may be because your mentee did not share anything worth exploring, or you may have missed it. Whatever the case, do not let that discourage you. When you run into these moments, don't worry! There are a couple of things that you can do to get a conversation going. The first thing you can do is ask them directly, "What is something that has been on your mind recently?" Or "What is something God has been teaching you?" These prompts can lead to good conversations over something that they have been thinking about recently.

If there is still nothing to talk about, this is a great chance for you to share something that is on your heart or that God has been teaching you. It's also an opportunity to bring up an area in their spiritual journey that you think needs growth. This is a moment where you take the initiative in the conversation and choose something to explore. Use this time to facilitate a more structured conversation over an important topic. Please take advantage of this opportunity. It is a beautiful chance to discuss theology, the character of God, challenging questions or stories in the Bible and so much more. Additionally, you can come prepared with activities or exercises to further their spiritual journey. Although this is a small section in the book, depending on your disciple, you should always be ready with something to talk to your mentee about when you meet with them. This is a chance for you to add structure to the meeting, so take advantage of it. If you are unsure what topic to choose, consider using supplementary materials, like Jim Putman's wheel, to aid your preparation. After you pose a topic and the conversation progresses, nothing else changes in the process. You will still be using the tools you have been learning; the only difference is you are the one who brought it up.

Depending on your disciple's spiritual maturity or the flow of your conversation, it may be appropriate for you to bring up topics relatively consistently. It provides additional structure that helps new believers learn accurate theology and how to follow Jesus.

As you think about potential conversation topics to discuss with your mentee, here are a few ideas to consider.

- The character of God
- The work of the Father
- The deity of Christ
- The work of Christ

- Who is the Holy Spirit?
- The work of the Holy Spirit
- Spiritual giftings
- How to abide in the vine
- How to pray
- How to read Scripture
- How Scripture came together
- Hearing the voice of God
- Discerning spirits
- Dying to the flesh and being alive in the Spirit
- Breaking sin patterns
- Living above reproach
- Evangelism
- Using your talents for God's glory
- Getting involved in a local church
- Appropriate depth of theology for the maturity of your mentee

There are just a few of many topics that can and will come up in your time with your mentee, but I hope that these examples provide a few ideas that you can fall back onto. The conversation that you and your mentee choose to have, whether it comes up naturally or something you bring up, should be for the benefit of the mentee. Your goal is to find and facilitate a conversation that will help them grow in their relationship with God and live according to his Word.

It doesn't matter how you get there as long as it ends with a topic centered around God that you and your mentee can discuss! You can do this—I promise. It may take time and feel clunky at first, but with practice it will become second nature.

I would encourage you to take time this week and practice noticing what God has to say about the words and actions of your family, friends, coworkers, and strangers. At this point don't say anything, just listen and recognize what God has to say about what we do, think, and say.

I cannot wait to see the way God reveals to you his influence over every aspect of life! As you notice your own and others' actions, you will see a better picture of our depravity and God's plan for our redemption.

Best of luck practicing and seeing how God moves!

11

Digging for Treasure

When I was eleven years old, I had what I thought was the greatest idea of my lifetime—to bury treasure in my backyard. I found my blue piggy bank filled with twenty dollars of loose cash, grabbed a shovel, and headed outside. I started toward the woods with a spot in mind, the backside of a pine tree that was on the edge of the trail. I dug a hole about a foot and a half deep and gently set my piggy bank inside. After filling the hole, I marked it with an X by laying two small twigs over it. Two years later, one summer day, I decided to take my brother, who was six at the time, on a treasure hunt. After making up a longwinded story about why there was treasure in our backyard, we set out to find it. I made up clues as we went to keep him invested, but eventually he grew frustrated with me. On the verge of losing my treasure-hunting buddy, I took him to the tree, and to my surprise, the two twigs I placed there two years ago were nowhere to be found! After digging aimlessly for a while, my brother started to lose hope that there was anything there. I assured him there was, but no matter where

I dug, we couldn't find it. To this day, my blue piggy bank is still in the ground, but my brother doesn't believe it.

I will never forget that day because I learned that searching for treasure is hard and not always successful.

Treasure hunts take time and exploration. As you check in with your mentee and notice areas that you can dive deeper, you are still at the start of your quest, and it is going to take some exploring and figuring out clues to get to a conversation that leads to treasure—life change.

In this journey, your primary tool for digging is asking questions. At this point, we have talked about the basics of questions, but here we'll take it a step further. Asking good questions helps your disciple explore their thoughts and feelings. It shows them that you are interested and can even help them explore other areas they haven't thought about yet.

Now before you get nervous about asking questions, I promise that you are already better at it than you know. You ask questions all the time! "How are you?" "What are you up to?" "What are you thinking about ____?" Questions are a natural part of life. Don't let fear keep you from doing something you already know how to do. There isn't pressure to ask the perfect question. As long as you keep the end goal in mind, you will be fine. Remember, the goal is to point them toward Jesus. Our questions should aim to help them explore how the Lord fits into their life. If you keep this in mind, asking questions is just a matter of combining a few words together!

As we learn to ask questions and "dig for treasure," we need to remember that it takes time. Helping your disciple see something from God's point of view can be a process. Life is complicated, and it may take some detangling to understand the heart of the issue. Questions help us untangle the craziness of life and allow our mentees to explore their thoughts and feelings in a way they don't normally get to.

We can ask two types of questions; these are formally known as open-ended and closed-ended questions[1], but we can think of them as the "let's explore" questions and the "tell me the facts" questions. Exploring questions are unique in that they do not have yes or no answers. These questions allow our mentees to clarify thoughts, explore new things, unravel messy situations, and find direction.

Let's Explore!

Exploring questions are a true gift to our mentees because they encourage our mentees to continue talking and explore their thoughts and feelings. Asking these kinds of questions is a big part of the "treasure hunt" and having life-changing conversations. What is unique about exploring questions is that the goal of them is not to give advice or find a solution; it is to help them explore further.

We use exploring questions to understand our mentee's thoughts, feelings, and actions. Exploring questions allow them to process things and can help you gain traction in a conversation. These types of questions are essential to helping transform their heart, head, and hands!

Thoughts: Questions centered on thoughts focus on what your mentee thinks about or what their opinion/perception of something is. Questions about thoughts are helpful because they give us insight into your mentee's thinking processes. Understanding the previous knowledge your mentee has on the conversation will help you fill in the gaps or explore misconceptions they may have about Scripture. Questions that are focused on their perception of something will give you insight into the state of mind of your mentee. Understanding your mentee's internal dialogue will help you to see areas for growth or change. Your mentee's mental state is a huge opportunity for growth and for conversations about Jesus. A few examples of questions on thoughts are:

> "What do you think the word forgiveness means?"
> "What stuck out to you in that passage?"
> "What do you think the Bible says about that?"
> "What were you thinking when they said that?"

Questions focused on thoughts are great prompts for talking about the transformation of our heads (knowledge/mindset) and of our hearts (beliefs).

Feelings: Questions about feelings are focused on two areas of feeling: their reaction about something that God says or their response to an event. If we are honest, there are challenging verses in the Bible. Jesus' call for our life is big and difficult to follow. Asking questions focused on their reaction to a passage may help you catch a glimpse into their internal state. For example, if they say, "it's not fair that God calls me to forgive my brother," that lets you know where their heart is on forgiveness and allows you to help them understand God's call for us to forgive. Questions focused on how your mentee feels about something may help your mentee process what is happening in their life. Processing gives them a chance to express their emotions and sort out what is what. Questions about feelings also give you insight into areas you may need to work through such as jealousy, anger, unforgiveness, complacency, etc. Notice how your mentee is feeling and use questions to further explore the conversation. Below are a few examples of questions on feelings:

> "When Jesus says ____, what's your gut reaction?"
> "How does that make you feel?"
> "I know it can be hard to love our families sometimes. As we talk about it, how are you feeling?"
> "It sounds like you had a pretty difficult conversation. How are you feeling now?"
> "Tell me more about that; how were you feeling when she said that?

Questions that are focused on feelings can lead to great conversations that are centered on our hearts and our minds, but usually, they are more focused on our hearts.

Actions: Questions about actions are the easiest and most straightforward of exploring questions because they are the most tangible. Questions on actions can be focused on either what they did or what they could or should do in the future. Questions focusing on what they did can relate to any action but most often relates to sinful actions, praiseworthy actions, or actions they took while in a leadership position. These questions are a great time to reflect on what happened and what they did well or what they did poorly. During questions on actions, notice areas to praise them in as well as areas where they can grow in leadership. Questions about current actions usually lead to questions about future actions. Future-oriented questions can help your mentee create a plan to avoid sin, grow in leadership skills, or even take action in a place they have not before.

For example, you can use a future-oriented question on sharing the gospel to encourage your mentee to share the faith with someone next week. Below are a few examples of action-oriented questions.

> "Oh wow. What did you do next?"
> "How did leading small group go last week?"
> "That's so cool that you went to talk to her. How did it go?"
> "What do you think God would call us to do in that situation?"
> "How do you think we could create a plan to avoid doing that again?

Action-oriented questions are great for promoting and continuing conversations focused on the transformation of our hands. It is a great opportunity to steer a conversation toward helping our mentee live out the gospel.

Tell Me More

Besides asking questions about thoughts, feelings, and actions, there are two other types of exploring questions: ask them to keep talking or ask for clarification. Asking them to keep talking can be thought of as "tell me more" questions. For these types of questions, you aren't asking about anything in particular. You are simply asking them to elaborate on what they are talking about. This can be helpful if your mentee doesn't tell you the full story, you are looking for more details, or you want to flesh out an idea a little further. Asking for clarification is used when what your mentee is saying doesn't make sense or is not the full story. Asking for clarification is helpful for mentees who like to ramble or struggle to tell a cohesive story. Below are a few prompts you can use to ask them to tell you more or to clarify.

"Tell me more about ___."
"Elaborate more on ___."
"What do you mean by that?"
"I'm sorry; I'm not following. What happened?"

Give Me the Facts

I want you to think about "give me the facts" questions as a tool that you can use to gain clarity on a situation. Give me the facts questions are used to help us gain information that we were either missing or need to gain clarity on. They are not to be the primary tool in exploring with your mentee. They don't have the depth behind them to hold a conversation. If you use give-me-the-facts questions as the central tool in your conversation, it will fizzle out quickly. If you don't believe me, try to answer this question for more than two minutes: "Do you have a brother?" For most people, their answer will not last more than a few words. If the conversation were to continue on that subject, it would require an exploring question like, "tell me how you and your brother get along." Give-me-the-facts questions are best used to seek clarity.

Okay, that was a lot of information, so let's take a moment and zoom out. Before I say anything else, please do not get lost in the weeds. I know it can seem overwhelming and hard to remember everything, but hear me when I say that when it comes to asking questions, it is not about remembering the details. Asking questions comes down to intention. If your intention is to help your mentee explore what is happening in their life and to point them to Christ, you are doing great.

How to Ask Exploring Questions

At this point, we have gone through the nitty gritty of asking questions so let's move on to the practical application.

As we think about asking exploring questions, the key is to keep them short and simple. People have trouble answering multiple questions or lengthy questions. They may feel like they don't know which part to answer or may even forget about part of the question. Focus on one area of the problem/story at a time. For example, asking your mentee, "How did teaching go? Were you nervous? What did you talk about? What did the pastor say?" all at once is overwhelming. They won't be able to answer any of the questions fully and it will take away from your time with them.

When asking questions, it is important to keep the question focused on the individual. It is fruitless to ask questions about what someone else was thinking unless that helps develop the conversation further, which is rare. Focusing on your mentee also helps you avoid a debate about what "actually happened." Your focus is on your mentee's perception of the event, not what "actually happened." Facts are important, but are not the focus.

When it comes to phrasing the question, keep your question open-ended. Rather than say, "Were you mad when they said that?" Say, "How were you feeling when they said that?" The best way to keep exploring questions that are open-ended is to try and use "what" or "how" stems for your question. A few examples of templates that you can use are: "How did that___?" "What were you___?" "What do you think___?" or even "Tell me more about ___." Tell me more is not a question on thoughts, feelings, or actions, but a request for them to share more with you about something. From these templates, you simply need to add the right subject to the question to make it specific to the conversation. For example, if your mentee is struggling to get into the Word consistently you may ask, "What are some barriers that are keeping you from reading?" Or "What about reading has been challenging for you?" Notice both questions are focused on exploring and understanding.

It is essential to note that your questions should move your "treasure hunt" forward. You are looking for gold, a conversation centered around how Jesus interacts with their life. If you are on the right trail, don't change the topic. Stay focused on that topic until it runs dry. Keep looking for a way to relate Jesus to their lives, and once you find it, don't stop!

Helpful Tips for Exploring
- Keep it short and sweet.
- Err on the side of empathy and compassion.
- Keep the questions open-ended.
- Ask questions for understanding.
- Ask yourself: How can I change a statement to a question?
- Use what and how stems.
- Rely on exploring, not factchecking.
- Perception is more important than facts.
- Focus on their thoughts, feelings, or actions.

- Ask yourself: how does God fit into the picture?
- How can you help them see this through the lens of Jesus?

These tips will help you to stay on track with your disciple and help them process. Remember, your mentee is not looking for the perfect question, and neither should you. Just do your best! Asking questions is something that comes with practice. You cannot become an expert at it overnight. Keep working at it, and I promise you will get the hang of it! If you are wondering how this kind of conversation looks in real life, below is a conversation I had recently with one of the men I mentor.

Sample Conversation

As you read this conversation, notice the use of questions. The conversation flows naturally and helped him to expand on his thoughts/feelings/actions.

Kyle: How's your young adult group going?
Owen (not his real name): It's been all right. Honestly, I've really been struggling with it lately.
Kyle: Oh, tell me about it. What's been going on?
Owen: I mean, nothing is wrong, but I've been frustrated with the leader recently. He keeps telling me he wants me to lead but isn't giving me the chance.
Kyle: That must be really frustrating. I know how much you care about that group. Could you tell me more about it?
Owen: I keep offering to lead a small group, but he says I'm too young and that he's scared I'll say something dumb.

Kyle: I can imagine that must hurt. You guys have known each other for a while.
Owen: I've never given him a reason to distrust me. I don't know why he thinks that way.
Kyle: I'm curious. Do you think there is anything that would change his mind?
Owen: Not that I can think of.
Kyle: So, the unfortunate news is that we can't force him to trust you or convince him of something, but I'm wondering if there are still ways to lead.
Owen: I'm not sure. He really won't let me do anything.
Kyle: Have you ever heard of servant leadership? It's the model that Jesus uses.

This conversation led to an important truth about what it means to serve, and it all started by asking simple questions. If you look at the questions asked, they were not complex, nor did they ask groundbreaking things. They were simple and touched on the most important parts of what he was saying. By identifying the most important piece of information that they touched on and asking a question about it, they can expand on the topic and explore their thoughts more.

Asking questions can be scary and a little awkward at the beginning. I want you to know that it is okay to make mistakes. Your mentee does not need the perfect question; as long as you are on the right track, they will usually go with it. Remember to focus on the most important part of what they are saying and to focus on their heart, mind, and hands.

12

When You Hit a Rock

When I started working in ministry, I had the perspective that, above all, I should love others. My primary goal was to make people feel cared for and supported. After all, isn't God all about love? The way I evangelized, taught, and discipled was influenced by this mentality. As I met with men, I demonstrated love by listening to them and asking questions, but I stopped there. I thought that if I made them feel cared for, encouraged, or supported, I had done my job and was a good mentor. We left every conversation feeling great, but after a year or so, I realized the folly of my nature. My mentees had plateaued and were living in the same faulty beliefs they started with.

I realized that my perception of love was wrong. I thought I needed to encourage and love my mentees at all times. But always "loving" my mentees actually harmed them. My unwillingness to challenge them harmed their spiritual walk. I realized it was more loving to correct and rebuke them at times than it was to keep my mouth shut. I had to realize that discipleship, and Christianity for that matter, is not about being "nice"; it's about seeking godliness. Proverbs 13:24 tells us, "Whoever spares the rod hates their children, but the one who loves their children is careful to discipline them." Withholding correction from our mentees is not loving. Scripture tells us that means we hate them. That may sound extreme, but our fear of correcting hurts their relationship with God. It is more loving to correct than it is to be "loving."

In the last chapter, we talked about understanding what our mentees are saying. If you are at a place where you can understand why they are feeling the way they feel, you are doing a great job. This is significantly further than most conversations go, and it is a blessing to your mentee to be understood by you. Now I want to push us beyond understanding to seek transformation. We need to push beyond "walking a mile in their shoes" because, unfortunately, that doesn't lead to life change. We want to help them see life from a broader perspective—God's perspective. I believe the story of Job demonstrates the importance of changing perspective. Throughout the story, Job's attitude toward God changes. Job starts on the right track and remains righteous throughout, but as time passes, Job grows contempt for God. Job gets angry with God and demands God answer for the injustices against Job. God, in His graciousness, answers Job, but not in the way Job expected. God puts Job in his place by revealing the magnitude of who He is. There are three chapters dedicated to God's response where God shows Job a glimpse of His power. God asks Job if he was there when the mountain goats gave birth, if he makes the sun go across the sky, and so much more. God shows Job the full picture.

God helps Job zoom out and see the world from a different lens—His lens. This is our goal as mentors: to help our mentees see the world through God's lens. If we only see the world from our point of view, we will struggle to live God-centered lives. As you listen to your mentee, try to help them see things through the eyes of Scripture. We want to help our disciples interact with the world with a Jesus-centered lens. If something they are saying, doing, or thinking does not add up with Scripture, you have the chance to offer biblical truth to the situation. Seeing through God's lens is crucial to our relationship with our disciples and is the stage where we truly begin to help them model their lives according to the ultimate objective truth, God's Word. By helping our disciples understand their world more fully and understand their thoughts and actions, we can better look at the internal reasoning for why they are doing what they are doing. This allows you to see how their thoughts, actions, and feelings align with Scripture.

As you see how your mentee's thoughts align and don't align, you could point your disciples toward objective truth and, by doing so, not only work on changing external behavior but work on transforming their hearts to be more like Christ. When you meet with your disciple, your goal is not only to give good advice. If our goal is to only give good advice, we have fallen short. Our goal must be to give advice centered through the lens of Scripture to make our disciples more like Jesus. Simply offering advice doesn't lead to deeper relationships with Jesus. We must use this opportunity to help them gain a deeper understanding of Christ and transform their lives to look like His. When challenging discrepancies using Scripture, you can use similar wording on your challenges. You may feel that you can challenge discrepancies better by saying a variation of "what does the Bible say about that?" or "what do you think Jesus' reaction would have been?" By challenging within the context of Scripture, we not only ground our disciples in Christ, but we also are able to work out of objective truth. Remember, our role as disciples must be to have them become more like the teacher (Luke 6:40). If we fail at this role, we have fallen short of our goal as a discipler. This does not mean that every single one of your conversations is going to have a Bible story or even include Scripture. This does mean that everything we do should be through the lens of the Holy Spirit.

When Things Don't Align

As you help your disciple see their life through the lens of Christ, there are inevitably going to be areas in their life that won't align with Scripture. When you see areas that don't align with Scripture, you have the chance to offer guidance by challenging them to realign to Christ. When you challenge them, your goal is to help them become more aware that what they are doing does not align with the Bible or what they believe. When challenging, point out discrepancies between what Scripture says, what they believe, and what they are doing.

For example, if the person you are mentoring believes that a man should love his wife like Christ loves the church but often gets angry and yells at her, you can help him see that those actions contradict what Scripture says. Challenging in this way helps your disciple take responsibility for their thoughts/actions. Challenging nudges disciples out of denial, helps them see their problems differently, and encourages them to take responsibility.

Let's take a look at an example of something that we could gently challenge. Allie prides herself on her willingness to serve other people and help them, but every time she is asked to get involved in a project, she says no. Susan, Allie's mentor, recognizes this and, during one of their meetings, poses cautiously, "Allie, it sounds like you are saying that you love to serve other people but every time you're asked you decline it. Why do you think that is?"

As you may imagine, Allie may feel challenged by Susan's question and become defensive. One of the biggest tasks in this stage is finding a way to challenge where your disciples feel supported instead of attacked. Everyone has defenses. This means that when we challenge discrepancies, it's important that we have finesse. With challenges, you want to indicate an area of the person's life that is incongruent with Scripture. Remember, few people like being challenged, so we need to challenge strategically. Challenges should be done cautiously, gently, respectfully, thoughtfully, and with empathy and be balanced with support.[1] It's important that you are cautious not to make judgments when you challenge someone. A challenge should be an opportunity for them to explore and understand themselves more fully. If you judge them, you may embarrass them or make yourself seem better than them. Look at a couple of examples of how you could start a challenge.

- On the one hand ____, but on the other hand ____.
- What you are saying doesn't seem to align with Scripture.
- You say ____, but you are doing ____.
- I'm hearing ____, but I'm also hearing ____.

Let's take a look at an example of challenging to see what this looks like in a real conversation.

Dave (Mentee): Jim, I just feel like I have no quality friends. I am really looking to find people that I can live life with and grow in Christ, but I can't seem to find anyone that really understands me.
Jim (Mentor): That is wonderful that you are seeking fellowship, Dave. I'm curious, why do you feel like no one understands you?
Dave: I feel like nobody wants to have deep conversations. Every time I'm with my friends we just end up going to the gym and playing basketball. We never really get the chance to talk.
Jim: So it sounds like you're longing for something deeper than superficial friends.
Dave: Yes! I want deep friendship, but no one here is like me. I keep waiting to have deep conversations with these guys, but it never seems to happen.
Jim: Dave, have you ever tried starting a conversation about Jesus with them?
Dave: Well no. . . . I was waiting for it to come up.
Jim: Dave, on one hand, you say you want deep relationships and fellowship with others, but on the other hand, you aren't willing to initiate the conversation. How could you ever expect to dive deep if you never bring it up?
Dave: You're right. I'm just scared to.

Jim pointed out a discrepancy in Dave's words and actions. Dave wanted deep relationships but wasn't willing to try and start them. Jim caught onto this and cautiously challenged Dave. The challenge led to a deeper conversation with Jim, where they talked about the importance of taking an active role in fostering community.

As you experience opportunities to challenge your mentee to follow the Lord, your challenge must be receivable. A challenge is not helpful if it is not received. If what you say falls on deaf ears or your mentee gets defensive, it is unlikely that positive change will result. You need to find a way to challenge them so that they hear you and feel supported instead of attacked. It is important to note that this will look different for each person. Some of the men that I meet appreciate honesty and directness when I challenge them. I can't beat around the bush, or they won't understand or get frustrated. With other men I meet, I have to challenge them while encouraging them. I have to use a "compliment sandwich" where I compliment them, then challenge them, and then compliment them again. It helps to soften the blow for them and allows them to listen to me more clearly. There are many ways that you can challenge someone. It's up to you and your disciple to find out which way is most effective for them.

A Note on Correction

One of the biggest pushbacks I have on challenging is that "Christians should not judge." In light of that pushback, I want to take a moment to address judgment in the Christian walk. A proper understanding of correction is essential to the spiritual development of an individual. Let's look at Hebrews 5:11–14 to look at an example of challenging a group of people to grow.

> We have much to say about this, but it is hard to make it clear to you because you no longer try to understand. In fact, though by this time you ought to be teachers, you need someone to teach you the

elementary truths of God's word all over again. You need milk, not solid food! Anyone who lives on milk, being still an infant, is not acquainted with the teaching about righteousness. But solid food is for the mature, who by constant use have trained themselves to distinguish good from evil (Hebrews 5:11–14).

Notice the way that the author speaks to his audience. They acknowledge that the audience is not where they should be. They should be mature in their faith by this time, but they are mere infants. The audience has not grown up as they should, and the author is clear about where they stand in their maturity. The author is blunt and to the point. He doesn't sugarcoat his response, nor does he soften it by talking around the problem. He addresses the problem head-on. The author's willingness to acknowledge the weaknesses of his audience may make you feel uncomfortable. If so, that's okay. Challenging can be nerve-racking at times, and it's all right to be nervous. In fact, when we challenge, it is best to err on the side of caution. The problem becomes when we sway too far and begin to think correction is wrong.

Correction is good and biblical, but unfortunately, the water between correction and judgment gets a little bit murky sometimes. Thus, it is important that we gain a good understanding of what biblical correction is.

The word for "judgment" in Koine Greek is *krino* which means "divine judgment." *Krino* can give a verdict that has either positive or negative consequences. When we judge someone, we are "banging the gavel" and making the "final call" about things we do not have the right to. We are not the judge. Rather, God is the judge as He is the only one that is truly just. Judgment is different from correction, though. The word correction is used in 2 Timothy 3:16, "all Scripture is God breathed and useful for teaching, correcting, rebuking and training in righteousness." The word for correction is *epanorthósis*, meaning "correction, reformation, setting straight again."

To correct someone is to set them straight again. Our goal in correction is not to place judgment on them or their actions; rather, it is to help straighten them out again. Think about yourself when you were a kid. I'm sure you can think of a time when you were misbehaving and doing something you knew you shouldn't. When your parents caught you, they corrected you and, depending on the severity of what you were doing, disciplined you. They didn't discipline you because they disliked you or were judging you, or wanted to see you suffer. They corrected you and, at times, disciplined you out of love. The Bible says in Hebrews 12 that God disciplines those He loves. Correction and discipline are a natural part of love and growing up. Without being disciplined, we will never be able to grow up to maturity. We need people to set us straight, and we need to set other people straight sometimes so they can grow to be mature in Christ. To correct, rebuke, encourage and help somebody develop in maturity in Christ is essential to their faith walk. That may mean it's uncomfortable sometimes and hard to correct, but it's worth it. We only correct those we love and are invested in. Your disciple knows that you love them and that you are investing in them by looking out not only for their happiness and well-being but also for their spiritual maturity, even if it requires correction.

Judgment in the Christian faith is not acceptable, but correction and reproof are! Don't let a faulty perception of judgment hinder you from helping your disciple be more like Christ.

Final Note

When you challenge someone, you have the opportunity to help them take corrective steps. Helping our disciples reorient back to Christ is just as important as helping them see their error! Don't lose sight of the end goal and spend all your time on correction. After they realize that what they are doing doesn't match up, transition to corrective measures. There are numerous ways to help your disciple get back on track. Whatever method you choose, make sure it is collaborative. Work together to make a plan that they are willing to follow. If they aren't willing to be corrected, take a step back and try to find another way to help them see their error.

Now that we have learned how to dive deeper into a conversation and "knock out a rock in the way," we are going to take it a step further. We are finally at a point in the conversation where we have struck gold. At this incredible point in the conversation, we get to take a more active role and assist our mentees. In the upcoming chapter, you are going to learn the five tools of every mentor: cheerleader, challenger, teacher, dreamer, and connector. Each role is essential to helping your mentee mature into who Christ has created them to be. I am so excited for you to read the next chapter. It is, in my opinion, one of the most empowering and exciting parts of being a mentor, and I hope you find it as fun as I do!

13

Striking Gold

If you've made it to a point in your conversation with your mentee where you have attentively listened to them, noticed a topic worth exploring, and then explored the topic with them, take a moment and congratulate yourself. You are doing a great job! Getting that far in a conversation is not easy and takes a lot of work! You're providing a space to speak and making them feel heard. Seriously, if you can do this well, you are a true blessing to your mentee. What I want to do now is push you one step further. Being understood and feeling cared for are wonderful things, but they don't necessarily lead to life change. Our end goal of mentorship cannot be understanding; it must be sanctification: to become more like Christ. If we lose sight of this goal, discipleship loses its purpose. We must keep our eyes centered on assisting our mentees in their journey to become like Christ. This requires a changing of roles in the relationship.

Thus far, we have primarily talked about listening skills and how to ask questions. In this next stage, however, we get to assist our mentees by utilizing the skills, knowledge, and wisdom that we have learned throughout our time pursuing God to help them become more like Jesus.

This stage in the conversation is what most people imagine discipleship relationships to be like; a mentor sharing the wisdom and biblical truth they have learned to help their mentee. The problem with this image is that we blow it way out of proportion. When I talk to people about the potential of mentoring someone, I am always astonished at how much they expect themselves to know. They expect to be some wise sage that has a Bible verse for everything. This would be nice, but it is not realistic. Assisting our mentees in the sanctification process does have to do with knowledge, but it is far more diverse than being able to pass a Bible quiz.

Whether you feel prepared or not to assist your disciple, I believe this chapter will be beneficial for you to read. Because, in all honesty, assisting is far simpler than we make it out to be. We help others all the time! We help people make choices, encourage people, teach, and offer advice on a daily basis. Assisting is something we do naturally, so I am confident you can do it in your mentee's spiritual walk as well.

The Five Roles of Every Mentor

To make this seem more obtainable, we can break it down into five manageable roles. These roles come from the communication field and aim to cover the broad roles of mentors. The five roles of every mentor are 1) cheerleader, 2) challenger, 3) teacher, 4) dreamer, and 5) connector.[1] As we explore these roles, we will gain a better understanding of what it means to be a discipler.

If you have trouble committing the five roles to memory, you can use the following acronym to help you remember.

Cheeleader   **C**an
Challenger   **C**reate
Teacher   **T**he
Connector   **C**omplete
Dreamer   **D**isciple

1. The Cheerleader

One of your primary roles as a mentor is to cheer your mentee on in their walk with Christ! You are their biggest fan and their number one supporter. As their cheerleader, you get to encourage them in their walk with Christ, notice and affirm all the wonderful qualities you see in them, and speak truth into their identity. As their cheerleader, you should always be looking for opportunities to encourage your disciple in

Cheerleaders
Affirm your disciple genuinely. People can easily smell fluff!

their walk. Being a cheerleader means you are encouraging whether or not things are going well. Imagine if the cheerleaders of a football team stopped cheering when their team was losing—it wouldn't be very encouraging, would it? Regardless of the situation, speak life into your disciple and encourage them!

Throughout Scripture, multiple prominent disciple-maker plays the role of a cheerleader. Paul is a cheerleader throughout his epistles. If we look at the beginning of many of Paul's letters, we see him encourage the church to whom he's writing. First Thessalonians is an example of how Paul encourages the church of Thessalonica:

> For we know, brothers and sisters loved by God, that he has chosen you, because our gospel came to you not simply with words but also with power, with the Holy Spirit and deep conviction. You know how we lived among you for your sake. You became imitators of us and of the Lord, for you welcomed the message in the midst of severe suffering with the joy given by the Holy Spirit. And so you became a model to all the believers in Macedonia and Achaia. The Lord's message rang out from you not only in Macedonia and Achaia—your faith in God has become known everywhere. Therefore, we do not need to say anything about it, for they themselves report what kind of reception you gave us. They tell how you turned to God from idols to serve the living and true God, and to wait for his Son from heaven, whom he raised from the dead—Jesus, who rescues us from the coming wrath (1 Thess. 1:4–10).

Paul intentionally encouraged the believers and spoke life into the church, affirming their good qualities. Notice that Paul doesn't fluff up his encouragement. He is specific and affirms them genuinely. As a cheerleader, affirm your disciple genuinely. People can easily smell fluff. If you give someone a general compliment that isn't from the heart, they know you don't mean it, and the compliment falls flat.[2]

Types of encouragement. As we talk about becoming a good cheerleader, I want to take a moment to talk about what makes a good cheerleader. Dr. Joel Wong is an associate professor of counseling at Indiana University that studies encouragement.[3] Through his research, he developed a system of encouragement that will aid us in our quest to be good cheerleaders. He breaks down encouragement into two types: "Challenge-focused" encouragement and "Potential-focused" encouragement.

Challenged-focused encouragement is employed in a difficult situation: "I know things look really bleak right now, but I know you have the strength to get through it." Encouragement doesn't always mean positive things are happening. In this way, you become a comforter-encourager, helping and inspiring them through hardship.

Potential-focused encouragement is affirming the possibilities available to them: "You're really good at communicating; have you ever thought about teaching?" This is more of a cheerleading encouragement affirming them, their skills, and their personhood.

Tone is also a huge part of encouragement. If you want encouragement to stick with someone or mean something, it matters how you deliver it. A halfhearted compliment won't stick. Allow your words of affirmation to come from the heart, and be specific about the positive things you see.

Aspects of encouragement. The way we encourage matters. Whether we are using challenge or potential-focused encouragements—or just saying "You're great!"—the delivery matters. Good delivery is the difference between brushing it off with an easy "nice" and a meaningful comment that pushes them forward. There are three factors to a strong delivery: who says it, how they say it, and its sincerity.

Who says it. The willingness to accept praise depends on

the relationship. Lighthearted compliments from strangers such as, "I like your shoes" may be accepted without a second thought. But imagine if a stranger said, "The way your heart beats for the weak is beautiful; I see Christ in you in moments like that." You would be taken aback and not sure how to respond! As a mentor, you have a unique position in the mentee's life. You have a wonderful opportunity to encourage and love, but don't jump the gun. Your encouragement matters, but ease into it. Allow the relationship to develop before diving too deep too fast.

How you say it. The way you phrase your encouragement is important. When you encourage or compliment your mentee, make it matter. If you smoosh it between critiques, rush through it, or don't give them the time to receive it, you are doing them a disservice. When you encourage, be intentional. Create an environment that allows your mentee to receive and embrace what you've said.

Sincerity. If you don't mean it, don't say it. An disingenuous or forced compliment will damage your relationship. It will bruise your trustworthiness and make them less likely to accept what you have to say later on. When you encourage, tell them what you see—not what you think will make them happy. Replace extravagance with honesty. Speak from your heart; it will go further and mean more.

Ways of encouragement. There are always opportunities to encourage—in nearly every conversation, you have multiple opportunities to encourage! Whether you are encouraging them for their performance in their high school football game, comforting them after a breakup, or speaking to who they are becoming, you have the opportunity to encourage them. There are three primary aspects of encouragement that you can use to help us become better encouragers:

What They Do. Affirming someone for what they do is the easiest form of encouragement because it is observable. If your mentee did well on a test that you know they studied hard for, affirm them, and tell them they did a good job. If they were promoted at work, cheer them on. As you look for ways to encourage them in what they're doing, consider focusing on the fruits of their labor, the effort they put into something, a skill/talent they demonstrated, a struggle they overcame, something new that they tried, or a leap of faith that they took. Whatever they did, find a way to intentionally praise them for it!

Who they are. This is your chance to affirm the positive qualities they have now. What values do you see in them that are admirable? What character traits do they have that remind you of Christ? What do you see in their heart? Sometimes affirming who they are is a simple shift in language from what they did to who they are: "You did a great job teaching" vs. "You are a great teacher." You are speaking to their heart, not their hands. Focus on what their best qualities are and notice the qualities that they are developing. Focus on who they are as a person.

Who they're becoming. This is the most powerful form of encouragement. Affirming who someone is becoming can be life-changing. I will never forget the moments when my mentor looked me in the eyes and told me who he sees me becoming. As you speak life into someone, you want to focus on qualities that you see them developing but are not fully developed yet. As you cheer them on, focus on the kind of person they could become and the incredible things you could see them doing. Help them see the impact that can have for the kingdom of God. Often what you see God doing through them is much bigger than what they see. Help broaden their horizon to the incredible person that they are becoming. Cast a vision that they can grasp.

As you think about these three areas, be aware you will most likely transition between them frequently. Each category can be a stepping stone to other ways of encouragement.

Types of encouragement[4]

Challenge-focused	Potential-focused

Aspects of encouragement

Who says it	How they say it	Is it genuine?

Ways of encouragment

What they do	Who they are	Who they're becoming

2. The Challenger

The challenger is typically the role that causes the most anxiety for mentors—usually due to a misunderstanding of the role. Many people stereotype the challenger as a "Type A" kind of person who will speak the truth no matter the cost. Although some mentors may challenge this way, it's not the only way to challenge. It is important that we understand that any challenge is only as good as its ability to be received.

The ways you challenge can be diverse. It can be a difficult conversation, asking hard questions, keeping your mentee accountable, keeping them focused on their goals, or gently showing them their sin. The role of the challenger varies depending on the situation and the mentee. As a coach, I've learned that a challenge is only as good as the player's ability to receive it. There are some players that I can be straightforward with and others where I need to implement the good old "compliment sandwich." The effectiveness of my coaching and my challenge is only as good as their ability to hear what I am saying. As you challenge your mentee, you need to challenge them in a way that they will receive it.

Paul's letters are full of challenges. In them, we see his desire for the churches to whom he's writing to mature and become more like Christ. Let's look at Colossians 3 to see an example of Paul challenging the church to develop in their faith.

> Since, then, you have been raised with Christ, set your hearts on things above, where Christ is, seated at the right hand of God. Set your minds on things above, not on earthly things. For you died, and your life is now hidden with Christ in God. When Christ, who is your life, appears, then you also will appear with him in glory. Put to death, therefore, whatever belongs to your earthly nature: sexual immorality, impurity, lust, evil desires, and greed, which is idolatry. Because of these, the wrath of God is coming. You used to walk in these ways, in the life you once lived. But now you must also rid yourselves of all such things as these: anger, rage, malice, slander,

and filthy language from your lips. Do not lie to each other, since you have taken off your old self with its practices and have put on the new self, which is being renewed in knowledge in the image of its Creator. Here there is no Gentile or Jew, circumcised or uncircumcised, barbarian, Scythian, slave or free, but Christ is all, and is in all. (Col. 3:1-11)

Paul challenges the church to set their minds on things above and to rid themselves of sin. His challenge is straightforward and focused on helping the church grow up in Christ: by "setting their minds on things above" and rid themselves of sin. Paul pushes the church to become the best version of themselves and live as if the new kingdom is already here. Notice he does not appear to be angry. In fact, he is not even corrective! Paul's challenge is a call to grow in the faith and live out the lives they are called to live. Challenging does not always require us to be corrective. Sometimes it can even come in the form of encouragement.

As we think about challenging others, I want to acknowledge that it can be scary. It's scary to confront someone about something they are doing wrong. We fear hurting their feelings, ruining a relationship, or having them get angry with us. As we step into challenging our mentees it is important that we understand what we should correct others on—and what we shouldn't. We do not have to challenge every single thing we see room for growth in. It takes discernment to know when to say something and when to be quiet.

What you choose to challenge your disciple on should depend upon their needs and what will be effective for their growth. A challenge should always be to the benefit of the disciple even if it hurts them in the moment. Remember, your mentee's spiritual health is more important than their feelings getting hurt. As you think about areas worth challenging, it is important that we understand what is worth challenging. Some areas to consider challenging your disciple in are: spiritual disciplines, relationships with others, living in sin, not using talents, or emotional immaturity. Your goal is to help them self-reflect and see things through a different lens.

I've always appreciated the way Paul challenges because he changes depending on the situation. In some instances, Paul is straightforward and doesn't pull any punches. In these moments Paul's vigor and tenacity simultaneously inspires and terrifies me. An example of this is in Paul's correction of Peter in Galatians 2. Paul is sharp and to the point because he knew that's what Peter needed. In other instances, Paul is gentle. In Acts 17 Paul is gentle in his salvific message to the people of Athens because he knew he could share the truth with them by meeting the Athens church where they were.

Worth challenging: Spiritual disciplines, relationships with others, living in sin, not using talents, and emotional immaturity.

Paul's methods differ depending on who he is talking to. He is aware that a confrontation is only good if it is received. This is something that I am still learning. When I was a part of a ministry that furnished international students' apartments, I had a group of volunteers who helped me with the moves. There were a few incredibly consistent volunteers who were lifesavers for me and my physical well-being! But there were times when we ran into problems. Sometimes furniture would not fit in doorways, or we would miscommunicate how to move something. In those moments when things were not going well, I needed to know how to talk to my volunteers. I knew one of them listened best when I was direct and assertive. I could be somewhat stern in those moments because it is what helped him and us succeed. Another volunteer would have cried if I corrected him that way, so I knew I needed to be gentler and encouraging when our move wasn't going well. This is a lesson that I've learned the hard way and have messed up on more occasions than I would like to count, but I am continually learning that everyone responds to challenges differently, and as a mentor, it is our job to find the best way to challenge them.

Challenges can be direct confrontation or indirect confrontation. Direct confrontation is the way I talked to my first volunteer. Direct confrontation is exactly what it sounds like. If you choose to confront your mentee directly, you need to let them know where they went wrong and what they can do to work through it. This can be scary, and it requires discernment and finesse. You want to speak clearly without insulting or demeaning your disciple. A rule of thumb is to enter the conversation cautiously, give them the benefit of the doubt, and keep their best interest in mind. Focus on the situation or event rather than their character. You always want to challenge what they did, not who they are. Give them time to respond and be open to hearing what they have to say. The confrontation will likely lead to a deeper discussion. Personally, I hate direct confrontation, but because it helps some of my mentees grow, I have to suck it up and challenge them directly.

Direct confrontation may be uncomfortable at times, and that is okay. Sometimes correction hurts, but it is worth it. I prefer indirect confrontation. Indirect confrontation is helping them realize their own faults through asking questions, using analogies, and exposing flaws in thinking. The general rule of thumb in challenging indirectly is to help them explore the situation and incorporate truth when appropriate. Some of the skills used in indirect challenges are active listening, asking questions, analogies, pointing out discrepancies, and helping them think through the situation. These skills take practice and come with time.

3. The Teacher

As you and your disciple live life together, you can teach them. This is an opportunity for you to share the insight and knowledge you have learned over your time as a Christ-follower. You can speak the truth and add clarity to Scripture and life! What an exciting opportunity!

As you read that last sentence, you may not have had the same thoughts about this being an "exciting opportunity." In fact, it may have scared you a little bit. You may believe that you don't know enough to teach anyone or that you're still a beginner. It's okay to feel that way. There is nothing wrong with not knowing the answer to something. One of the best things you can do when you don't know the answer is say, "I don't know, but let's find the answer together." This humanizes you, and your disciple will feel more comfortable asking questions.

Being a teacher is far broader than a pastor preaching or a small group leader sharing. Teaching does not require a stage or even a large audience. You only need an audience of one. At its essence, teaching is all about sharing knowledge about something. You can teach someone about anything! You've most likely taught someone something in the last week or two. Whether you taught someone how to use the tv remote, updated them on the scores of last night's football game, or explained a passage of Scripture to them, you taught them. We teach and are taught all the time. But we sometimes make it complicated when it comes to Scripture. The only thing that is required of us when we are teaching is to share what we have learned or experienced over the years.

There are a few qualities of effective communication that if we understand will help us to teach others more effectively: Clear, Accurate, and Real—CAR!

> **C***lear:* Does it follow a logical progression? Does your main point make sense?
> **A***ccurate:* Is it factually true? Is your point grounded in the Word?
> **R***eal:* Is what you are teaching meaningful to you? How has this truth impacted you?

Following CAR keeps us on track and allows us to teach effectively without confusing ourselves or our mentees by trying to hit too many points in a teaching moment. You do not have to be a professional teacher or emulate great orators. Just be yourself! Share how the passage has impacted your life and the truth that Scripture holds. CAR is a simple checklist that helps us remain grounded and teach effectively. Regardless of your personality or teaching style, you can always aim to be clear, accurate, and real.

4. The Connector

As the connector, you are your disciple's "agent." Your goal is to connect your disciple to other people you know will help your disciple reach their goals. As their mentor, you may have connections to other ministries, churches, or teachers that will be helpful for your disciple to be a part of. You want to help them get connected in multiple areas so that they can get experience and learn from a variety of people. Do not be selfish and keep your disciple to yourself. They can learn a lot from other people and those people may thrive in different skills than you do. By networking and creating relationships for your disciple you provide them with the opportunity to grow in a way that you could not provide by yourself.

One of my mentees was trying to figure out what career path he wanted to take. He had a few different options he was considering and wanted my input. Throughout the years I've had minor training on helping people with career choices, but I didn't know much. Instead of giving him my opinion, I connected him with my friend Cathy. Cathy has been in human resources for forty years and is an expert in helping people discern career paths as well leading leadership development training. She was the perfect person to connect with my disciple. As they met, they developed a good relationship, and Cathy was able to help him find a career path that worked for him. Sharing your disciple and connecting them to others is a crucial part of being a good mentor.

In *The Mentoring Guide*, Vineet Chopra gives three reasons that our disciples should meet with other people as well. 1) If disciples do not meet with others, it limits their growth and ability to learn from different approaches, styles, and strategies from others; 2) it makes the mentee reliant on you for everything; and 3) it limits your growth as a mentor to learn from other people's knowledge. By connecting our disciples to others, we not only help them grow but we also prepare them to become self-sufficient by becoming connected to a bigger community.[5]

Paul utilizes his role as a connector primarily through his disciple Timothy. Timothy is sent by Paul to Thessalonica, Corinth, and Ephesus. We see in 1 Corinthians 4:17 that Paul sends Timothy to Corinth to remind the Corinthians of Paul's teaching, as well as to Thessalonica, in 1 Thessalonians 3:2–3, and finally to pastor at Church in 1 Timothy. Paul connects Timothy to the churches for the churches' growth and the believers' encouragement.

Connect your disciples to others. It will lead to a fuller experience for them and will help them develop in the faith more than if you solely met with them. I have three mentors I meet with on a regular basis. Each mentor offers something different to me that I do not get from the others. One offers wisdom, another teaching, and the other connections. Each mentor helps me in my walk with Christ, but in a different way. I would not be where I am today if I only met with one of them. Be openhanded with your disciple and connect them to others who can help them grow.

5. The Dreamer

As a mentor, you also get to dream with your mentee! This kind of dreaming has nothing to do with sleep but everything to do with who they could become, what they could do, what their passions and how they could pursue them! This dreaming has a purpose and direction. When we dream with others, it allows them a peek into the kingdom impact they could have or the person they could become. When we dream with others, we help them find direction and motivation.

Direction and Motivation

Imagine with me that you won a free, all-expense-paid trip to anywhere in the world with two of your best friends. As the three of you sit down to talk about the vacation, what is the first thing that you need to know before planning the rest of the vacation? The destination, of course! The rest of the vacation is determined by the destination that you choose. It would not make sense to bring swimsuits to Alaska or learn French to travel to Spain. The rest of your trip is determined by where you decide to go!

When we dream with others, we give them the chance to "choose their destination." Dreaming provides a place of freedom where they get to look at their life and say *this is who I want to become*, or *this is what I want to do*. Having a clear understanding of who we desire to become and what we aspire to do gives us the motivation to take action. We must be able to answer these fundamental questions to pursue what our heart is longing for. This truth is a common occurrence in all of life. You were willing to take action to pursue or invest in your spouse because you saw an outcome, marriage. You attended college with a degree in mind because you had an idea of the impact you want to make.

Finding Direction

As a mentor you have the beautiful opportunity to help

your mentee find the desires of their heart. You can facilitate their exploration by helping them *visualize a destination, think bigger* and *throw off doubts* keeping them from exploring.

The first step in dreaming is helping your mentee visualize a destination. This is done by asking future-oriented questions that explore what they would like to do or the person they want to become. Some examples of these kinds of questions regarding character are: "When you're on your deathbed what do you want to be remembered for?" "What kind of spouse/parent do you want to be?" "What are three characteristics you want to be known for?" Focusing on qualities and characteristics that reflect Christ is a great start to developing direction for character-related conversations. You can also ask questions about what they want to do. A few examples of these types of questions are: "If you could do anything, what would you want to do?" "What does your heart break for?" "If you were to do something radical for God, what would it be?" Questions focused on action can help mentees start to see their role in the kingdom of God.

As they talk about their dream, ask questions. Ask them to describe it for you. What does it look like? What would they do? By encouraging them to imagine it more fully, the dream begins to become more lifelike, and they begin to see themselves in the picture. The goal in asking questions about the dream is not to make them do it, but for them to see the impact they can make.

The second step is to help them think bigger. In my experience, I have found that people shortchange themselves when they dream. Talented and wonderful individuals that I meet think their ability to make an impact in the kingdom of God is small. I believe this is a result of us downplaying our own abilities. To think bigger, challenge your mentee to trust God to equip them. Do not let them get caught up in themselves, push them to think of themselves as capable of making an impact.

Finally, work to throw off doubts they are having. Although there are many reasons that doubts emerge, they are usually a result of being focused on logistics when it comes to dreams. Your mentee may be focused on: time, money, location, competency, changing life plans, etc. When they get stuck on logistics, remind them dreaming isn't about making it happen right away, but about exploring what God has placed in their hearts.

A great way to overcome doubts and explore more is by using the word *hypothetically*. *Hypothetically* takes away the pressure to act and allows freedom to think. It creates a freedom where, for a moment, there are no restrictions on life. By thinking hypothetically, we allow our minds to explore and dream about something they are passionate about without being worried about taking action. This helps not only to put logistics to the side but allows the mentee to speak from their heart.

As the desires of your mentee's heart emerges, it is natural that they want to do something about it. When we see a vision or set a goal, we want to work toward it. This is a wonderful thing, rejoice in the excitement that your mentee has!

As their vision and direction emerges it is important that you handle the situation well. Like all short jolts of passion they tend to dissipate if not cared for well. A sudden jolt of energy to read the Bible in a year quickly fizzles out without proper structure. With this being said I am not advocating that you and your mentee create an action plan of how to achieve their goal. Doing so defeats the purpose of dreaming. If our goal was to make action plans, we never truly gave our mentee a chance to dream without consequence.

Harness their passion by talking to them about how they can see themselves becoming the man or woman God has called them to be. Focus on developing character and leadership ability. This way their passion can be harnessed without losing steam. A clear direction of God's call for our life with a strong passion to seek him leads to a life on fire for the Lord.

As you and your mentee talk about their passions, a great way to check if they are on the right track is to look backward into your disciple's life to see if what they have done in the past lines up with what they want to do in the future. For example, one of the young men I meet with wants to create a gaming-centered ministry. He is creating a platform to play video games with others as he invests in them. He has always loved technology and video games and is getting a degree in computer science. In high school, he felt the gaming community was one that was overlooked by society, and he wants to change the culture. His past aligns with the goal that he is aiming to achieve now. Talk with your disciple to see if their goal is something their past has been building them up for. This is often a good test to see if it is truly what their heart yearns for.

Caution: do not make a five-year plan with them; your goal is not to map out their life! Rather the goal is to dream about the future. One of my favorite verses about dreaming is Proverbs 16:9, which says, "The man sets his course, but the Lord guides his steps." I love this verse because in

God's goodness he allows us to choose our goal, but he is our GPS along the way. God orchestrates the twists and turns of life and reaching your goal does not always work out the way you expect. Things change, and God opens and closes doors. Our goal in dreaming is not to create a plan, but to start heading in a direction. God is going to give directions as we go.

As you think about dreaming with your mentee, please note that there are a lot of ways to dream with them, but the central theme behind every method is that our dreams should be from the heart. Proverbs 20:5 says, "The purposes of a person's heart are deep waters, but one who has insight draws them out." It is out of the heart that our purpose arises. As you dream, draw from the heart not the mind. Be willing to explore different ways to dream with them. There isn't a one-size-fits-all way to dream with someone. Do whatever allows them to think freely and dream from their heart. Be willing to live in fantasy with them. Encourage them to dream without restrictions. Listen and encourage their dream even if the dream may never become a reality. It is through those dreams that we gain direction and motivation toward what is next in life. Dream big! It is a chance to see what makes your mentee's heartbeat.

The Harm of Failing to Dream

Personally, dreaming is the hardest thing for me. I am a realist and see things from a logical perspective. In the past when people I've mentored have come to me with their dreams, I've unintentionally shut them down. I asked far too many logistical questions and told them to slow down and think about it. I now realize that was a mistake. Rather,

I should have dreamed with them and vision casted what their dream could look like.

Recently, a young man I mentored came to me with the idea to create a daily podcast reflecting on Scripture. When he told me about it, he was thrilled; he was all in! As a realist, I knew he didn't have the time for it. He's incredibly busy and it was going to be a huge operation. In the nicest way possible—at least I thought so—I tried to help him see how much time it would take and that he did not have time to do it. I could tell that he was disappointed by my response. He wanted me to dream with him and I didn't. Later, I was reminded of a passage. First Thessalonians 5:19 says, "Do not extinguish the spirit." This verse tells us not to diminish or ignore the work of the Holy Spirit. How do we do this? By ignoring the Spirit's voice, not creating space for Him to speak, and living in sin.

As I reflected on this verse, I have often thought that it only related to me. I shouldn't quench the Spirit in my own life. But I began to wonder if I could quench the Spirit in someone else. Is it possible that my actions or words could put out the fire they have for God? I believe I did exactly that with this young man. I challenged him instead of dreaming with him. Don't quench the Spirit's fire in someone else by responding sharply; be someone who's willing to encourage them and even toss some more fuel onto their fire!

The Most Misused Skill

Now that we've discussed the five roles of a mentor, I want to bring to our attention a skill that is overused and often misused. This skill is known formally as "disclosure of similarities," but I like to think of it as the "same here" skill. The "same here" skill is sharing something you went through or someone you know who went through that is similar to what your mentee is going through. If you have ever been in a situation where you share something that you are going through, and the person you are talking to says, "Oh that happened to me as well and I fixed it by ___. You should try that too!" Or even worse: "That's not *that* bad, you should hear what happened to ___."

You know how frustrating it can be. I truly believe that many use this skill with good intentions, but it can easily be misused. It is infuriating to be sharing what is happening in your life, and someone responds by telling a story about themselves. This skill is misused when it takes the focus off your mentee and puts it on somebody else. When this happens, it diminishes the mentee's feelings, makes the mentee feel like you do not understand, and gives the impression that you are offering unsolicited advice. To "connect" with their mentee, a mentor can unintentionally hurt the relationship and ruin rapport. This skill can be beneficial when used properly—but is to be used very sparingly and only when the attention is directly turned back to your mentee.[6]

Take a look at an example of the "same here" skill being used by Sarah and Pam as they talk about the challenges of being a new mother.

> **Sarah** (Mentee): "It's been so challenging, and I'm so tired. I feel like I never get to sleep, and I feel so overwhelmed."
>
> **Pam** (Mentor): "Yeah, it is a lot. I remember how crazy it was taking care of Tyler, Ashley, and

Becca at once. I know one is tough but three is unbearable."

Sarah: "I just feel like there aren't enough hours in the day to get everything done, and my husband has to work late, so I feel like I don't have a support system."

Pam: "Yeah, when Becca was born, my husband traveled a lot, and I spent countless nights home alone. It was a really hard time."

As you look at this conversation you may not think anything of it, but you should. Pam didn't help Sarah at all or even make her feel heard. Pam's responses were directed toward herself to "relate," but all it did was keep the conversation at a standstill. This is an example of a milder misuse of this skill, but I have seen far more egregious errors. Focusing on yourself or your experience can ruin your disciple's trust in you to dive deeper.

Your role in the "same here" skill is never, and I repeat *never*, to take the attention off your mentee. Don't change the conversation to make it about yourself—it isn't about you! If you share about yourself, your goal is to make them feel like they aren't the only one with the problem or to make them feel understood.

Here's an example of what an appropriate "same here" skill can look like.

Andrew (mentee): "I've been struggling with a pornography addiction for a long time. I feel like I'm trapped, and that God is mad at me."

Wyatt (mentor): "I hear how much it's weighing on you. Throughout my life I've struggled with a pornography addiction too, and I know not only how frustrating it can be but how embarrassed I was too. I'm so sorry that you are going through this."

Andrew: "Yeah. I feel embarrassed and ashamed of myself. Every time I watch pornography, I feel like God hates me."

From here the conversation continues and Andrew can expand on how he is feeling and about God's grace. What Wyatt does well in this situation is talk about himself and share vulnerably without taking the attention off Andrew. Wyatt shared how he felt, which helped Andrew dive deeper. You can share your experience as long as your goal is to make your disciple feel more comfortable and facilitate the conversation. Your goal here cannot be to talk about yourself or to solve their problem.

When you are meeting with your mentee, take a moment to check if you are using this skill to help them explore and feel known or using it to talk about yourself. If you are using it to talk about yourself, you need to recenter and focus on your mentee. If you use these skills correctly you will make your disciple feel heard, and help to explore the conversation further. If you use them incorrectly you will damage the relationship and make it hard for them to feel like they can open up.

What It All Boils Down To

We covered a lot of material in this chapter, so I want to break it down into the simplest form to avoid confusion. Your role as a discipler is to be intentionally invested in the life of your disciple. How you invest in them will look different for each person, but your goal is to walk through life with them–cheerleading, challenging, teaching, dreaming, and connecting.

(14)

Reaping the Reward

As you read the final chapter, I want to thank you for all of your hard work. You've learned a lot in the last thirteen chapters! You've learned how to find a mentee, set boundaries, understand the roles of discipleship, learned how to listen, and even how to assist your mentee. Thank you for taking the time and effort to seek God's call to make disciples.

The final component in a conversation with your mentee is what I like to call reaping the reward. You've struck treasure and are in the midst of a conversation centered on God, but now you need to make it stick. Assisting our mentees is wonderful, but, unfortunately, it does not always lead to life change. Sometimes mentees need help getting the truth to sink in or to take action. This is where reaping the reward comes in. The goal of this section is to help your mentee move forward with what they've learned.

It is natural that when thinking about moving forward that we should focus on action, but this is not always the case. I would like to show you a passage that has greatly impacted my perception of taking action, my walk with

God, and how I mentor others. This passage completely shifted the way that I help others take action. The passage is Matthew 7:16-20.

> By their fruit you will recognize them. Do people pick grapes from thornbushes, or figs from thistles? Likewise, every good tree bears good fruit, but a bad tree bears bad fruit. A good tree cannot bear bad fruit, and a bad tree cannot bear good fruit. Every tree that does not bear good fruit is cut down and thrown into the fire. Thus, by their fruit you will recognize them (Matthew 7:16-20).

Why did this well-known passage impact the way I mentor? Because I realized it isn't about the fruit! So many times I've read this passage and asked myself, "Am I producing fruit?" While this is a good question—and we should be producing fruit—there is something more to the passage. The important part of the parable is the tree. The passage tells us that good trees produce good fruit and bad trees produce bad fruit. But this truth is not reciprocal, good fruit does not produce good trees nor does bad fruit produce bad trees. The tree is more important as it is out of the health of the tree that it produces good fruit. God cares more about the tree than the fruit it produces. The produce that the tree bears is simply the product of the tree. God cares more about our heart than He does our work. The heart is the thing that needs to be transformed first, and then and only then will our actions follow suit.

In my life I have seen the folly of trying to produce fruit without focusing on the tree. For so long I tried to quench my earthly desires and live a good Christian life, but my heart was full of evil. In my mind, I was doing the right thing because I was producing "good" fruit, but my heart was far from God. The "good" fruit that I produced was forced and didn't last. It wasn't until my mindset changed to seeking heart transformation first that I began to produce true fruit. This fruit was natural. I didn't have to force it. This realization of pursuing heart change changed the way that I met with others. Instead of focusing on their external actions, I begin to focus on their hearts. Instead of telling them not to swear or to read their Bibles more, we talked about the issues of their heart. It felt weird, but the more we talked about their hearts and their relationships with God, the more external action came. I pray this is a moment of realization for you, too, to focus on trees rather than fruits. I promise it is worth it.

Give them a takeaway

Leaving a conversation with a clear plan and steps for growth helps our mentees progress and holds them accountable.

With that being said, whether working on the heart of the tree or the fruit, it is important that we help our mentees move forward in their relationship with God.

Leaving a conversation with a clear plan and steps for growth helps our mentees progress and holds them accountable. I try to follow the same motto when I speak: always give them a takeaway. My goal is to show them their need for the Lord, help them understand the character of God more fully, or give them practical takeaways that they can apply to their lives. In my opinion, there is nothing worse than telling someone to do something but not giving them any steps to do it. It's like telling someone to do a math problem without giving them the formula to solve it. When we are in a conversation with our mentees, we don't want them to walk away confused about their next steps. If your mentee shared a problem or admitted an area they have fallen short in, they've been vulnerable, and they may feel weak or exposed. Nobody likes feeling this way. In these moments we need help and comfort to get on the right track. There are many ways that we can help our disciple, but one of the most trusted ways is goal setting. Setting goals gives the mentee an opportunity to practice and work toward a new objective, seeking the Lord. Having goals in mind can motivate your disciple to take action and help them come to a deeper understanding of the truth you've uncovered.

Knowledge and insight must lead to action. If we do not take action as a result of knowledge or conviction, we deceive ourselves. See what James says about knowledge and action in James 1:22–24:

> Do not merely listen to the word, and so deceive yourselves. Do what it says. Anyone who listens to the word but does not do what it says is like someone who looks at his face in a mirror and, after looking at himself, goes away and immediately forgets what he looks like.

James says those who merely listen to the Word deceive themselves! They are like one who has forgotten what they look like after looking into the mirror. To listen to the Word without taking action is to deny the truth. Jesus speaks about the importance of taking action as well. As Jesus speaks about the final judgment, He makes a comment regarding the action of two servants upon his return. To the servant who has faithfully completed the tasks assigned to him, the Word says, "blessed is that servant . . ." (Matt 24:46) and that the servant will be put in charge of many. To the servant who has been unfaithful, the masters will "cut him to pieces and assign him a place with the hypocrites" (Matt 24:51). We should take these words seriously. The expectation is we take action and live righteously as a faithful servant.

Remember that your goal is to help your mentees see through the lens of Scripture. As you and your mentees make goals to move forward, remember the actions you take should be filtered through the eyes of Jesus or be centered on the disciple's relationship with Jesus. For example, if you are meeting with a mentee who already has a relationship with Jesus but feels far off, you may spend time discussing how they can grow in their relationship with Him. From there you may talk to your disciple about prayer and provide steps on how to grow in their faith. By providing action goals that are centered on building a relationship with God, you can help your disciple develop a stronger foundation in God.

Creating Goals

As we talk about creating goals, your disciple is the one pushing for the change. You cannot impose change on them. When an external force is pushing change, it's unlikely that true change will result. Think about a coach yelling at you to run faster. Their goal is to get you in better shape, but if you don't actually want to run, chances are you will only run hard when the coach is watching. It is only when people decide for themself that they are ready to change and are willing to take the difficult steps that true change will occur. It's the role of the mentor to help mentees change; the difference is in who is the driving motivation for the change.

Your mentoring goal is to create a supportive environment for them to explore the possibility of changing. When your disciple decides they are willing to change, they're more likely to take responsibility and ownership for their actions. Although you cannot be the one to make them change, you can facilitate a conversation that helps them realize not only their need for change but how to change.

Know that your disciple may not be willing to change right away. It may be a process with multiple setbacks. This is normal and is a part of the change process. As we think about creating action steps, we need to understand the different attitudes our mentees may have toward making change. Explore your mentee's attitude. If they are not ready for change or are still in denial, facilitating change will be like pulling teeth. Make sure that you and your mentee are both on board before diving in too deep.

Helping your mentee create steps toward change can be difficult. They may be defensive, apprehensive, or not willing to listen. I've had to learn the hard way that telling people what to do rarely works. I've been met with anger, defensiveness, accusations, and been called judgmental. Over the years, I have come to embrace these wise words from Blaise Pascal: "People are generally better persuaded by the reasons which they have themselves discovered than by those which have come into the mind of others."[1]

Many of us are persuaded to change when we think we have come up with the idea. As we mentor and help our mentees make changes to grow their relationship with

God, we need to keep in mind that they are most likely to receive it when they think it comes from their mind.

I want to be clear here: I am not advocating manipulating your disciple to change, it isn't ethical, and our mentees must learn to make choices for themselves. Rather, I am advocating for us to learn how we can best help our mentees make positive changes in their life.

The first hurdle to making change is overcoming your mentee's resistance. Unless your mentee is willing to change, you are wasting your time. If your mentee is unwilling to change, ask them why. Your mentee may be unwilling to acknowledge their error, will not repent of sin, intends to continue to live in sin, or hides sin from you. If your mentee has this attitude, focus on uncovering why they are okay living in sin and pray for conviction. Sin can be fun and over time we can become desensitized to it. Pray for the Lord to convict their hearts. Living in sin is not an option.

Ready for change

Many of us are persuaded to change when we think we have come up with the idea.

You may need to spend serious time working toward getting your mentee to a place where they are willing to accept that change is needed. If you are having trouble overcoming your mentee's resistance, I would encourage you to look at the way Jesus facilitates change.

Jesus helps people make change by showing them what they are missing. Throughout His ministry Jesus spoke about eternal life in the Father and what those who did not believe were missing. One example is found in John 4 and the woman at the well. Jesus cleverly reveals to the woman what she is missing—living water. The woman desires water that will never make her thirst again so she would not have to endure the shame and difficulty of getting water in the middle of the day. Jesus shows the woman what she is missing and as a result her life changes! The woman goes back to her hometown and proclaims the good news. We can help our mentees make change by showing them what they are missing. Your mentee may be missing out on the sweetness of an intimate relationship with Christ, the beauty of prayer, or whatever their sin is keeping them from. Helping them see that they are missing out on the fullness of Christ can help them make change.

Jesus helps people see their need for change by asking questions. Throughout the gospels, Jesus asks 307 questions.[2] Jesus asked questions to a wide array of people. He asked his disciples, pharisees, gentiles, government officials, and more. His use of questions engaged the crowd, created conversations, revealed error, and got people to think. For example, in John 6, after a particularly hard teaching, many of his followers left. Upon this, Jesus asked His disciples where they would leave as well. This was a turning moment for the disciples. Jesus gave them the option to walk away; it was up to them to decide whether they were willing to go all in. Jesus uses this question to push his disciples toward change. When people start to think for themselves, they come to their own conclusions on whether or not something is worth doing. Helping your mentee think about change will increase their conviction to take action.

Stories are a great way to help your mentee get off the fence and be willing to make change. Jesus uses parables all of the time. The Bible tells us that "He did not say anything to them without using a parable" (Mark 4:34). Throughout the gospels, Jesus uses over 30 parables to share the secrets of the kingdom of God. Jesus uses these parables not only to teach about what the kingdom of God will be like, but to facilitate change. This is seen in the story of Lazarus and the rich man, found in Luke 16:14-31. In this parable, Jesus shows the disciples that a life of luxury is nothing in comparison to our eternal destination. The rich man is sent to eternity in torment and Lazarus is given eternal life in heaven. This parable shows the importance of believing and living righteously. As the disciples hear that story, it may be possible that it steels them to hold strong to the faith. The use of stories can be a helpful tool in helping your mentee commit to making a change.

Jesus uses these tactics masterfully. Through this, the disciples grow in their faith and are willing to take action. As a mentor, you can use these tactics as well as create change. As we begin to discuss how to create a change, it is important to remember that our primary goal is to push our mentees toward God.

Our goal as a mentor is not to act as a counselor, life coach, or even offer good advice. Our goal is to help our disciples grow in their relationship with God. As you help your disciples make decisions and change behaviors and thoughts, it is not enough to offer good advice. Your primary goal in the relationship must be to point them toward God. Please don't lose sight of this fundamental truth of discipleship. We've talked about asking questions, listening, using reflective statements, making summaries, and helping make changes. These are wonderful skills and will help us in our conversations with our disciples, but they mean nothing if they don't point our disciples to God. Don't allow these skills to take over your mentor relationship.

Those skills are tools to help point others toward God, not tools to be used to replace God. Second Timothy 3:16 says, "all scripture is God-breathed and useful for teaching, rebuking, correcting, and training in righteousness." The Bible gives us all the words, stories, metaphors, and analogies needed to answer life's questions. Let's not strip God of His power to do a mighty work in the lives of the people we meet by rooting them in something that isn't Him. Psychology, sociology, counseling, and communication are all incredible fields and offer so much insight into the world and how our minds work, but they are not what we are working toward. I urge you to be cautious of using these tools too much. You already have everything you need in the truth of God's Word.

Creating biblical change can be difficult. There is not always a clear answer or action step to take. It requires discernment to create biblical and effective action steps.

The number one thing I tell mentors about creating action plans is that the plan has to be consistent with what is being discussed. Think about it like creating a workout plan for someone. If you were creating a workout plan for someone to develop their leg muscles, it wouldn't make sense to write a bunch of arm exercises into the program. The action plan should mirror the thing your mentee is trying to work on. For example, imagine Katie is struggling to get into the Word consistently. It would not make sense to talk about serving at a local charity; Katie needs help reading the Bible. An appropriate action plan would be to discuss ways that Katie could get into the Word. Solutions may include creating a Bible plan, accountability, helping Katie carve out time to read, and so forth. The plan is dictated by the area of interest.

As you spend time with your mentee, you will inevitably find many areas your mentee needs to work on. Following Christ's example is difficult, and we all have a long way to go. As you see multiple areas to work on, refrain from trying to work on all of them at once. Trying to change a lot of things at once is extremely difficult. If you focus on too many things at once, your mentee will likely be unable to implement any of the changes you discussed. Imagine you were learning how to decorate a cake, and your instructor tried to teach you how to use fondant, prepare icing, stack layers, create complex icing patterns, and add accessories all at once. You would be overwhelmed and unable to truly master any of the tasks and you would make little progress as a baker. In mentorship, the same principle applies. Trying to get your mentee to work on serving, praying, reading, evangelizing, refining character, resisting sin, etc. all at once is incredibly difficult. The result will be a mentee who is overwhelmed and unlikely to make true progress in a single area. Focus on one thing at a time. Spend time developing a firm foundation before moving on to something else.

Creating an Action Plan

As a reminder, creating steps to change must be driven by your mentee. They are the ones in control of their lives and can ultimately do what they want. The desire for change must come from them. Growth is facilitated by collaboration. The collaboration between you and your mentee to create goals is essential. If you create all of the goals and prescribe them to your mentee, you fail to equip them to think for themselves. Your goal is to help them figure out what is the best solution to their problem, not be their solution. Always offering solutions actually enables your mentee to remain stagnant and does not give them the ability to think/process things biblically. Helping them figure out what to do is a balance of encouraging them to think while guiding them as necessary.

There are numerous ways that you can facilitate change and make an action plan with your mentee. Honestly, I had difficulty condensing the material and figuring out the best way to convey how to create an action plan. After much deliberation, I hope I have found something useful for you.

I tend to approach creating action steps systematically. I imagine myself as a doctor trying to figure out what is wrong with my patient and find a way to fix it. If you were a doctor and someone came to see you with a broken arm, you would identify the problem and work with them to create a plan to fix the problem, i.e., getting a cast. In mentoring, we can follow the same approach. Imagine that your mentee's relationship with her husband is not going very well. She gets frustrated with him easily, and resentment is building. Forgiveness and self-sacrificial love are problem areas that she needs to work on. After identifying these areas, you and your mentee can work together to create an action plan that will help her love better. Examples of potential action steps may be talking to her husband about her frustration, problem-solving, sitting in the love of Christ, and so forth. Thinking this way can create clarity in the situation and help you and your mentee think rationally about the problem. The purpose of identifying the problem and goal is to facilitate smooth and relevant action steps. After the problem and goal have been identified, move toward creating action goals.

Moving beyond preparation is facilitated by the type of goals that you create. Your goals must be rooted in action, not thought alone. *Conviction without action is no conviction at all.*

Knowing how to create good goals can be difficult without a framework. Over the years, I have found SMART goals to be a helpful resource.[3] If you are unfamiliar with SMART goals, it is an acronym for five components of goal setting: Specific, Measurable, Attainable, Relevant, Time-based. If this acronym works for you, take hold of it and utilize it. It is a wonderful tool, and I hope it is useful for you. I believe that this acronym has fantastic value toward accomplishing physical/material goals such as exercising, sleep patterns, cutting down on smoking, etc. But the tool has limits on creating and achieving spiritual goals.

Of the five parts of SMART goals, measurable and time-based do not always apply to spiritual growth. Spiritual development can be intangible, unmeasurable, and unable to be constrained by time. For example, if your goal is to develop a more intimate prayer life, it cannot be measured easily. You could try and measure it by times prayed per day, but that can easily become legalistic and doesn't fully encompass a healthy prayer life. Trying to box spiritual development into measurable goals can create an unhealthy view of a relationship with God for your mentee. If "success" is measured by how often you do something or don't, you can create a legalistic view of the faith and unintentionally create a pattern of thinking that does not account for God's grace. Measurable goals may be appropriate when discussing leadership positions but should be done with caution. At times measurable goals can be helpful. For example, setting a goal of preparing for a small group the day before to ensure familiarity with the text. Measurable goals in leadership can be dangerous when they become numerical. Chasing numbers can compromise the integrity of the ministry, create competitiveness, and impact a church's willingness to challenge.

Time-based goals can be helpful for developing spiritual disciplines and taking action but do not apply to relational intimacy with God. Goals rooted in action, such as reading the book of John in a month, can give mentees something to work toward and be helpful in their faith walk. I have used weekly Bible plans to keep myself accountable for years. Timeframes may provide motivation for mentees to do something and overcome procrastination or laziness. Time-based goals do not translate well into relational aspects of the faith. Early on in dating my wife, I decided that I would know if I was going to marry her by our six-month anniversary. As six months came and went, I still was unsure. We didn't know each other well enough yet and we had a lot of growing up to do. The decision to marry her came over time and could not be rushed by a timeline. Our relationships with God are similar; it is impossible to quicken relational intimacy with God by putting a timer on it. It is through the genuine pursuit of the Lord and the prompting of the Holy Spirit that we can grow in intimacy with the Lord. Be wary when using time-based goals with your mentee. Relationships develop organically and need to be given the time to prosper.

As seen above, there are some challenges to using SMART goals in spiritual growth, but they can be a helpful tool. Try them out and see if they are helpful to your mentee's growth.

As you become more confident in helping your mentee

reap the reward, you may find yourself relying on SMART goals less. You will begin to create your own style that will fit the needs of your mentee. As I've grown as a mentor, I've stepped away from the SMART goals in favor of circling back to the question, "What does this person need to succeed in their faith?" This simple question helps keep me focused and motivated toward creating a plan with my mentee to help them grow in their relationship with God.

Now that you have created the action plan, the only thing left to do is implement it. You can help your mentee implement the change by holding them accountable. Accountability keeps individuals from straying away from the goals that they've set for themselves. Over the years, I've created many goals for myself. My mentor and I established action plans and talked extensively about how I could walk away from sin in my life or act more Christlike. On more occasions than I would like to admit, I fell short. After a few weeks of trying, I gave up and fell back into my sinful habits. My fleshly desires overtook my convictions, and I remained stagnant in the faith. Looking back, I wish I had communicated with my mentor more about my need for accountability. Our failure to do so harmed my relationship with God and allowed me to live in sin.

A good accountability system does three things: creates a space for forgiveness and confession (James 5:16), shares the weight of the burden (Gal. 6:2), and encourages your mentee to press on (Heb. 12:1–3).

A Space for Confession and Forgiveness

Regardless of the area you and your mentee are focusing on, it is inevitable there will be moments they fall short. They may fall into sin, become complacent in their faith, or lose sight of the mission. Whatever it may be, your mentee may experience shame and guilt for falling short. Holding them accountable means giving them a chance to share their failures and ask for forgiveness from the Lord for their sins. James 5:15–16 expresses the need for us to confess our sins to one another and that the prayer of a righteous person will heal them. Accountability creates a space for forgiveness to occur. You have the wonderful opportunity to facilitate forgiveness and help your mentee cast off the shame that they are feeling.

Sharing the Weight

You and your mentee are a team. You have a joint interest in seeing them grow in maturity in the faith. As their mentor, you will share some of the burden of growth with them. If your mentee is struggling to remain sexually pure with their significant other, you have a responsibility to help them overcome their temptations. This may look like praying with them before their significant other visits, calling or texting them late at night to remind them of their fight for sexual purity, or asking them the day after how it went. You have a vested interest in their success. Galatians 6:2 tells us to "carry each other's burdens, and in this way, you will fulfill the law of Christ." You have the honor and privilege of carrying your mentee's burdens and helping them seek Christ.

Pressing On

You play an important role as the cheerleader of your mentee. We have already discussed the role of a cheerleader in detail in chapter twelve but let me reiterate its importance. Following God can be challenging. In seasons of our journey, we may get tired or even lose interest. As a mentor, you have the privilege of helping your mentee keep going. You act as the fan cheering on the sideline as the runner presses on. You are there to help them move forward. This type of accountability is essential. Without it, your mentee may grow faint and lose steam. In my ministry, I've seen multiple men lose steam, and I failed to encourage them. Instead, I pushed them harder, only quickening the fatigue. Keep your mentee accountable by cheering them on to press forward.

Here are a few practical tips to help you create accountability:

> *Consistency*: Accountability should happen frequently. Without consistency, accountability can fall to the wayside, and your mentee can lose steam.
> *Create a safe space*: Make sure your reception of how they are doing is loving. Our mentees need to know it is okay to fail, and that they will not be judged.
> *Don't be shy*: At times, it may feel awkward to talk about certain sins, but you must overcome it. Your mentee's spiritual health is too important to negate accountability because you feel awkward.
> *Privacy*: When talking about vulnerable or potentially embarrassing topics, make sure you are in an appropriate place. It is not wise to talk about a pornography addiction in a crowded Starbucks.
> *Know your limits*: You are not in charge of your mentee's spiritual success. It is up to them to decide what they are going to do. Avoid creating

accountability that is overwhelming. Don't be a helicopter mentor and nitpick every area of your mentee's life.

If you follow these general guidelines, you will create an atmosphere that will facilitate accountability.

I understand this chapter, and this book for that matter, has a lot of information to consume. Please don't let the amount of information get in the way of the general truth of this chapter. If I were to boil this chapter down into one sentence, I would say, "find a way to help them grow in righteousness." That is the basic idea of reaping the reward. You've already done the hard part. All that's left is helping them make a plan to succeed!

In the past couple of years of full-time mentoring, I have seen these ideas play out in a beautiful way. I've seen countless examples of men and women seeking righteousness and growing closer to God as a result of accountability. I've seen ministries thrive and ministries fall as a result of accountability or lack of it. I believe from the bottom of my heart that you have the ability and tools needed to help your mentee grow. I hope this final chapter has shown you that you can do this. You have everything you need to be an effective mentor. You had it from the start. All that God needs from us to mentor is the Holy Spirit and obedience. The only thing this book has done is give you a few tools to use. Go out and use what the Lord has given you to make disciples who make disciples!

CONCLUSION

Let's Go!

If you've made it this far, thank you! I'm honored to share my thoughts, experience, and research with you. I hope you have gleaned something useful from the material and that you have been encouraged in the faith!

There is treasure to be found in every conversation, and you have the tools to find it. You've learned to listen, ask questions, seek understanding, dive deeper, assist, and even how to facilitate change. I am proud of you for your hard work; I know these tools can be challenging to learn.

I want to end by sharing one of the things I most frequently tell my mentees after conversations: "Now that we've talked, you're accountable to it."

Throughout Scripture, knowledge necessitates responsibility and action. Eli was held responsible to his sons' actions because he knew what they were doing and didn't stop them. The Israelites were punished and driven to Babylon because they refused to turn to the Lord despite knowing what to do. Knowledge always means responsibility. Think about it like attending a presentation at work or school. After you leave the presentation or class, you are held responsible for knowing the information. Imagine a student trying to convince their teacher that despite going to the lecture, they aren't responsible for knowing the information on the test.

For better or for worse, you no longer have an excuse not to disciple. You don't have the option to plead ignorance.

So, go! Take action. Reach out to someone, schedule a time to get coffee, go and make an impact on someone's life! You and I have an incredible calling to go and make disciples. It's too important of a call for us to waste any more time. Before you put down this book, reach out to someone and set something up. Don't put it off any longer! You can do this, I promise.

Best of luck digging for treasure!

With Love,

Kyle

Endnotes

Chapter 1
1. "New Research on the State of Discipleship," Barna Research Group, December 1, 2015, www.barna.com/research/new-research-on-the-state-of-discipleship.
2. Alan Cooperman et al, "Choosing a New Church or House of Worship," Pew Research Center, August 23, 2016, https://www.pewforum.org/2016/08/23/choosing-a-new-church-or-house-of-worship, 4–5.
3. Dietrich Bonhoeffer, "Costly Grace" in *The Cost of Discipleship* (Norwich, United Kingdom: SCM Press, 1959), 47.
4. Carl S. Dudley and David A. Roozen, "Faith Communities Today: A Report on Religion in the United States Today," Hartford Institute for Religion Research, March 2001 (Hartford, CT: Hartford Seminary), https://faithcommunitiestoday.org/wp-content/uploads/2019/01/FACT-2000-Report.pdf, 42–43.
5. Francis Chan, *Letters to the Church* (Elgin, IL: David C. Cook, 2018), 94–95.
6. George Barna, *Maximum Faith: Live Like Jesus* (Ventura, CA: Metaformation, 2011), 29.
7. Greg Ogden, *Transforming Discipleship: Making Disciples a Few at a Time* (Carol Stream, IL: InterVarsity, 2016), 24–39.
8. Caroline Beaton, "We're Wired to Take the Path of Least Resistance," *Psychology Today*, March 11, 2017, www.psychologytoday.com/us/blog/the-gen-y-guide/201703/were-wired-take-the-path-least-resistance.
9. "New Research," Barna Research Group, 11.
10. Warren Bird and Scott Thumma, *The Other 80 Percent: Turning Your Church's Spectators into Active Participants* (San Francisco: Jossey-Bass, 2011), 23–39.
11. Dietrich Bonhoeffer, "Costly Grace" in *The Cost of Discipleship* (New York: Macmillan Publishing, 1976), 47–48.

12. Greg Ogden, *Transforming Discipleship*, 21–39.

Chapter 2
1. Bill Hull, *The Complete Book of Discipleship: On Being and Making Followers of Christ* (Carol Stream, IL: NavPress, 2006), 51–72.
2. Rabbi Shaya Karlinsky, on Pirkei Avot chapter 1, Mishna 4, https://torah.org/learning/maharal-p1m4.
3. Bill Hull, *The Complete Book of Discipleship*, 69–70.
4. Ibid., 63.
5. Ibid., 68.
6. Greg Ogden, *Transforming Discipleship*, 24–39.

Chapter 3
1. "Occupations of the 12 Disciples," All About God Ministries, www.allaboutjesuschrist.org/occupations-of-the-12-disciples-faq.htm.
2. Mark 9:18
3. Matthew 16:4–11
4. That is possible, and it's wise to keep your eyes wide open for unhealthy relationship signs.
5. 1 Corinthians 1:11
6. Proverbs 12:15
7. 1 Tim. 5:8
8. Proverbs 27:6

Chapter 4
1. Greg Ogden, *Transforming Discipleship*, 80. Ogden observes a "four-stage preparatory process" in Jesus' discipleship. The basis for this model is twofold: 1) leaders have a goal in mind for their followers, and 2) They adjust their leadership style to the level of the individual/group. In this model, there is no "best leadership style," but that each leader must adapt to fit the needs of those they are discipling.
2. The Learning Square: Abraham Maslow,
3. Ogden Resource Here
4. Luke 6:7
5. Luke 9:13–17
6. Luke 10:9
7. Luke 10:4
8. Luke 10:5
9. Luke 10:3
10. John 17:11–16

11. John 17:18
Gordon Training International.

Chapter 5
1. Albert Bandura, *Social Learning Theory* (Englewood Cliffs, NJ: Prentice Hall, 1977).
2. 1 Corinthians 11:1
3. Kendra Cherry, "How Does Observational Learning Actually Work?" Verywell Mind, October 14, 2022, www.verywellmind.com/social-learning-theory-2795074#a-few-applications-for-social-learning-theory.
4. Ibid.
5. John 1:11–13
6. 1 John 3:1
7. 1 Corinthians 6:11
8. 2 Corinthians 5:20
9. 1 Corinthians 3:9
10. 2 Corinthians 5:21
11. 2 Corinthians 5:17
12. 1 Peter 2:24
13. 1 Corinthians 6:19
14. 1 Timothy 1
15. 1 Thessalonians 2:7–8
16. Galatians 4:18-20
17. 1 Timothy 4:12
18. Jack O Balswick and Judith K. Balswick, "Parenting: The Process of Relationship Empowerment," in *The Family: A Christian Perspective on the Contemporary Home* 3rd ed. (Grand Rapids: Baker Academic, 2007). 120.
19. Odgen, 109

Chapter 6
1. Jim Putman, *Real-Life Discipleship: Building Churches That Make Disciples* (Colorado Springs, CO: NavPress, 2010), 25–35.
2. 2 Corinthians 5:17
3. Titus 3
4. 2 Timothy 3
5. Matthew 4, Ephesians 6
6. 1 Timothy 6
7. 2 Peter 3:17b–18

8. 2 Peter 3:16–17
9. Matthew 6:31–33
10. Romans 12:2
11. Romans 10:10a
12. Ezekiel 36:26–27
13. Romans 8:1–17
14. John 15:4–5
15. 1 John 3:23–24
16. Ephesians 2:8–9
17. Matthew 25:23
18. Matthew 25:26

Chapter 7
1. Tony Dungy, Nathan Whitaker, and Jim Caldwell, *The Mentor Leader: Secrets to Building People and Teams That Win Consistently* (Carol Stream, IL: Tyndale Momentum, 2011).
2. *E3 Playbook* (Kansas City, MO: Fellowship of Christian Athletes, 2020).
3. Mark Dever, *Raising up Leaders in Discipling: How to Help Others Follow Jesus* (Wheaton, IL: Crossway, 2016), 100–101.
4. Abraham H. Maslow, *Motivation and Personality* (New York: Harper and Row, 1954).
5. Chris Jackson and Niger Ballard, "Over Half of Americans Report Feeling Like No One Knows Them Well," Ipsos Public Affairs, https://www.ipsos.com/en-us/news-polls/us-loneliness-index-report.
6. Barna Research Institute, *The State of Discipleship: Research Conducted among Christian Adults, Church Leaders* (Ventura, CA: Barna Research Group, 2015), 42.

Chapter 8
1. Julie Starr, *The Mentoring Manual: Your Step-by-Step Guide to Being a Better Mentor* (Harlow, England: Pearson Education, 2021), 44–61.
2. Ibid, 49.
3. Ibid.
4. LeRoy Eims, *The Lost Art of Disciple Making* (Grand Rapids, MI: Zondervan), 31.
5. Ariel Ervin, "Identifying Key Features of Mentor Self-Disclosure in the Context of Youth Mentoring," *The Chronicle of Evidence-Based Mentoring*, April 7, 2020, https://www.evidencebasedmentoring.org/

identifying-key-features-of-mentor-self-disclosure-in-the-context-of-youth-mentoring/.
6. Renee Spencer, "To Disclose or Not to Disclose?" *The Chronicle of Evidence Based Mentoring*, October 23, 2020, https://www.evidence-basedmentoring.org/to-disclose-or-not-to-disclose/.
7. Starr, *The Mentoring Manual*, 76–77.
8. Bill Mann, "Why Vulnerability Matters in Mentoring. Leading Tomorrow," Leadingtomorrow.org, December 12, 2018, https://www.leadingtomorrow.org/blog/the-need-for-vulnerability-in-mentoring.
9. Dever, *Raising up Leaders*, 98–100.

Chapter 9
1. Diana I. Tamir and Jason P. Mitchell, "Disclosing Information About the Self Is Intrinsically Rewarding," *Proceedings of the National Academy of Science* 109:21 (2012), https://doi.org/10.1073/pnas.1202129109, 8038–43.
2. Ibid.
3. Kent C. Berridge and Morton L. Kringelbach, "Affective Neuroscience of Pleasure: Reward in Humans and Animals," *Psychopharmacology* 199:3 (August 2008), https://pubmed.ncbi.nlm.nih.gov/18311558/, 457–80.
4. Tamir and Mitchell, "Disclosing Information."
5. Clara E. Hill, "Skills for Exploring Feelings" in *Helping Skills: Facilitating Exploration, Insight, and Action*, (Washington, DC: American Psychological Association, 2020), 169–171.
6. Mark E. Young, *Learning the Art of Helping: Building Blocks and Techniques*, 6th ed. (New York: Pearson, 2017), 64–70.
7. Gerard Egan, *The Skilled Helper: A Problem-Management and Opportunity-Development Approach to Helping* 5th ed. (Monterey, CA: Brooks/Cole Publishing, 1994).
8. Hill, *Helping Skills*, 107–126.
9. Gary Smalley, *I Promise: How 5 Commitments Determine the Destiny of Your Marriage* (Nashville, TN: Thomas Nelson, 2007).
10. Probably a rare line you'd start a conversation with, but hey—anything is possible!
11. Starr, *The Mentoring Manual*, 72–75.
12. Hill, *Helping Skills*, 151–177.
13. Jim Putman, *Real-Life Discipleship: Building Churches That Make Disciples* (Colorado Springs, CO: NavPress, 2010), 111.
14. Ibid.

Chapter 10
1. Scott Branson, "Using Questions in Counseling," Counseling.education, https://counseling.education/files/questions.pdf

Chapter 11
1. W. R. Miller et al, "Enhancing Motivation for Change in Problem Drinking: A Controlled Comparison of Two Therapist Styles," *Journal of Consulting Clinical Psychology* 61:3 (1993), DOI: 10.1037//0022-006x.61.3.455, 455–61.

Chapter 13
1. Joseph Madison, "Mentoring Styles: Types and Appropriate Use," Study.com, https://study.com/academy/lesson/mentoring-styles-types-appropriate-use.html
2. Y. Joel Wong, "The Psychology of Encouragement," *Counseling Psychologist* 43:2 (2014), https://doi.org/10.1177/0011000014545091, 178–216.
3. Ibid.
4. Ibid.
5. Vineet Chopra et al. "Six Rules for Mindful Mentoring" in *The Mentoring Guide: Helping Mentors & Mentees Succeed* (Ann Arbor, MI: Michigan Publishing, 2019), 19–27.
6. Hill, *Helping Skills*, 169–171.

Chapter 14
1. Blaise Pascal, *Pascal's Pensées* (New York: E. P. Dutton, 1958), 11.
2. Clara E. Hill, "Skills for Providing Support," *Helping Skills: Facilitating Exploration, Insight, and Action*, 5th ed. (Washington DC: American Psychological Association, 2020), 107–126.
3. George T. Doran, "There's a SMART Way to Write Management's Goals and Objectives," *Management Review* 70 (1981), 35–36.

Acknowledgments

To my wonderful wife, RaeAnne—
Thank you for your continued love and support throughout this process. I am so thankful that God gave me someone who not only puts up with my faults, but challenges me to seek godliness. May our lives model discipleship in all we do and be a testament to God's goodness.
I love you, RaeAnne, and am grateful for our life together.

To my good friend and editor, Ciara Sosnowski—
Your passion for discipleship and living out God's call for your life inspire those around you to live boldly for Christ. You live out discipleship in all that you do. Throughout this project your insight, input, and critique have helped me take a frankly messy project into what it is today.
Thank you so much for everything!

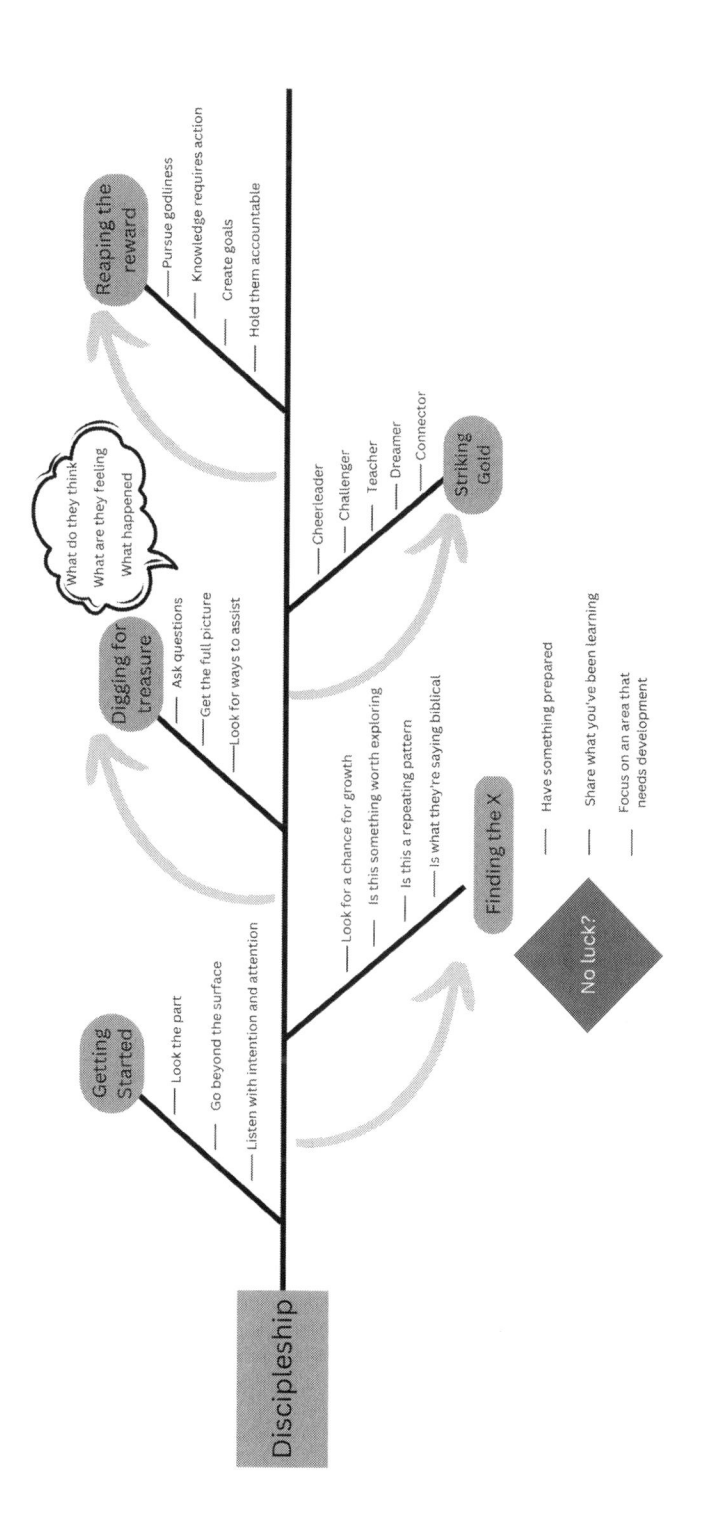

Discipleship

Getting Started
- Look the part
- Go beyond the surface
- Listen with intention and attention

Digging for treasure
- Ask questions
- Get the full picture
- Look for ways to assist

What do they think / What are they feeling / What happened

- Look for a chance for growth
- Is this something worth exploring
- Is this a repeating pattern
- Is what they're saying biblical

Finding the X
- Have something prepared
- Share what you've been learning
- Focus on an area that needs development

No luck?

Striking Gold
- Cheerleader
- Challenger
- Teacher
- Dreamer
- Connector

Reaping the reward
- Pursue godliness
- Knowledge requires action
- Create goals
- Hold them accountable

KYLE VENS is the director of Cultivate, a discipleship and leadership development ministry in Auburn Hills, Michigan. Since 2019, Kyle has mentored young men and women in their relationship with God as they grow and learn to use their God-given gifts for His glory. He has partnered with organizations such as YoungLife, InterVarsity, and Fellowship of Christian Athletes. Kyle has a passion for ministry and mental health. He believes that understanding someone's heart is essential to their growth. Kyle is finishing a graduate degree in clinical and mental health counseling at Oakland University, and he hopes to help people experience lasting healing from the true healer, Jesus.

Made in the USA
Monee, IL
15 August 2023

40857509R00129